MW00776027

Bible Study Guide
and Planner

own your life

Bible Study Guide
and Planner

Sally Clarkson

Whole Heart Press
Monument, CO

OWN YOUR LIFE
BIBLE STUDY GUIDE AND PLANNER
Published by Whole Heart Press
A division of Whole Heart Ministries
PO Box 3445, Monument, CO 80132

WHOLE HEART is a registered trademark of Whole Heart
Ministries, Inc.

© 2015 Sally Clarkson, Joy Clarkson
ISBN: 978-1-888692-29-7

Cover image: © asharkyu/Shutterstock.com. All rights reserved.
Cover texture: © pondkungz/Shutterstock.com. All rights reserved.

First Edition

Printed in the United States of America

Unless otherwise indicated, all Scripture verses are taken from the
New American Standard Bible,® @ 1960, 1962, 1963, 1968, 1971,
1972, 1973, 1975, 1977, 1995 by The Lockman Foundation. Used
by permission. (www.Lockman.org)

ALL RIGHTS RESERVED
No part of this publication may be reproduced, stored in a retrieval
system, or transmitted in any form or by any means—electronic,
mechanical, digital, photocopy, recording, or any other—except for
brief quotations in printed reviews, without the prior and express
written permission of the publisher.

For more on this book and author, visit:
www.SallyClarkson.com
www.WholeHeart.org
www.MomHeart.com

This study guide is dedicated to all the dedicated women who have attended one of my Mom Heart Intensive weekends in my home. Your friendship, encouragement, and commitment to own your lives and influence others for Christ fills my heart with love and joy.

Contents

— Foreword —

Own Your Life

Planting Your Garden

> *That person is like a tree planted by streams of water, which yields its fruit in season and whose leaf does not wither – whatever they do prospers.*
>
> PSALM 1:3 (NIV)

reminds me of "a life you don't need a vacation from"

who I want to be

"We should plant daffodils!" Joy's brown eyes were aglow and there was a dreamy excitement in her voice. With teas in hand, my youngest daughter and I were gazing out from the comfort of our living room on yet another thick March snowfall. Colorado winters can make one wonder if spring will ever come. That particular year we were beginning to wonder if we lived in C.S. Lewis's literary land of Narnia, where it was "always winter but never Christmas." Daydreaming and planning our summer garden brought warmth to our gray day.

Gardening in Colorado is an act of vision and intention. The good gardener must be able to envision the garden they desire, a difficult thing to imagine in the dead of winter! But if the gardener wants their little patch to bear fruit and be beautiful, she must have a plan. The high altitude, clay soil, and unpredictable temperatures require a gardener to anticipate the needs of her garden with insight and care if she wants it to be fruitful. One must choose the right plants, fertilize the ground, and water each plant according to its need.

I believe our lives are much like gardening in Colorado—they require vision, planning, and faith. It is no coincidence that the Bible speaks so often about life using the image or analogy of a garden or a field. Jesus taught the parable of the sower (Luke 8:4-15), and Paul's teaching reflected the same principle, "... for whatever a man sows, this he will also reap" (Galatians 6:7). Just as with a garden, the legacy of our lives will be evidenced by what we sow, cultivate, and grow. And even by what we uproot and remove.

In the realm of spiritual gardening, if you want your life to bear the marks of the kingdom of God, then you will need to tend it faithfully, and with faith. We can choose not to tend to the garden of our life, but when a garden is not nurtured and cultivated, it can become fruitless and vulnerable. The legacy of your life will be evident through what you plan, plant, nurture, and tend. Gardens grown when they are cultivated.

This Bible study guide and planner is intended to help you, as a faithful gardener, own your life—by reading and applying the Word of God in your heart, and by making a practical plan to live your life for God's purposes. Becoming a good gardener will involve three key components: vision, intentionality, and faith.

If I want to see daffodils peak their cheerful heads out in April, I must preemptively plant bulbs in September. In the same way, if I want to live a life that leaves a legacy of God's kingdom, I must be a visionary gardener, planting seeds that will become fruitful after years of faithfulness. Just as there is a vast diversity of flowers, so each person's vision for owning their life will be a little bit different, each involving different stories, strengths, challenges, relationships, and callings. Developing a vision for how you can own your own life involves praying and imagining with God what sort of legacy you could leave because of your commitments and decisions.

Once you begin to have a vision for your life, you must develop a plan to sow, cultivate, and maintain seeds of righteousness. As famous horticulturist L.H. Bailey wrote, "A garden requires patient labor and attention. Plants do not grow merely to satisfy ambitions or to fulfill good intentions. They thrive because someone expended effort on them." I hope that this guide will help you think through your vision for the legacy you will leave, and how you can implement practical plans to begin owning your life.

Being a good gardener of your life is fundamentally an act of faith. Every spring I marvel when the minuscule seeds I scattered in the cold ground the year before begin to burst from their wintery grave, growing into many shapes and colors of wildflowers. It is not a process I have a great deal of control over. The sun, seasons, and rainfall work their graceful magic; all I can do is plant my seeds and have faith that springtime will come.

So it is with our lives. Often our plans, daily sacrifices, and long term faithfulness can seem as though they are bearing no fruit. As we plan and do our best to plant seeds of faithfulness in our lives, we must remember that it is ultimately God who will cause the growth. As we own our lives and do our best to be faithful stewards of our little gardens, we partner with God as he causes growth and fruit. God gives us all the grace we need to be good stewards of our lives, and we must simply respond with faithfulness and faith that he will cause our gardens to bear fruit.

Every season of life is different. I hope that this planner will be a tool to help you think through and strategically own your life through many different seasons and years. I pray that the chapters in *Own Your Life* and in this planner will guide you in shaping your vision, developing your plan, and acting in faith as your own the life God has entrusted to you.

It is my hope that, just as I delight each year in the fruitfulness of a well-planned garden, you will have a life of beauty, growth, and fruit through taking ownership of your life for God's kingdom.

Own Your Life
Bible Study Guide
and Planner

— Chapter 1 —

Owning the Hero Who Lives inside You

Seeing Beauty and Purpose in Your Ordinary Days

Nobody really knows how smart or talented he is until he finds incentive to use himself to the fullest. God has given us more than we know what to do with.

SYDNEY J. HARRIS

One Wednesday as I was driving to physical therapy for my thrown-out back, I was already acutely aware of life's ambivalence for my plans and expectations. I had scrambled around the house looking in vain for my purse, and finally just got in the car without it, excited to steal a quick breakfast with Joy before my appointment. But the inconvenience didn't end there!

Somehow, on our way to a cafe we had been to many times before, we got lost in the labyrinth of downtown Denver crossroads. As I was turning down another wrong road, Joy was calling the theater where I thought I might have left my purse. No purse. My frustration made me want to throw my hands in the air with a dramatic, *"This morning is wasted!"* But I knew it wouldn't help, so I took a deep breath and we pressed on.

So often it can feel like weeks, months, and years of life can become an endless comedy of errors, rife with work, ear infections, bills, diapers, and a hundred other setbacks. And yet, when we focus on the chaos around us, we can forget to see the beauty and purpose God has for us in each stage of life.

There was a time in my life when my days were consumed in an endless cycle of mama-with-little-ones duties. It would've been easy for me to think during that season that my life wasn't very important, and certainly didn't rise to the level of radical Christian living. And yet it was in those hidden years that God was building and strengthening a foundation of love, faithfulness, and fruitfulness. The books I read to my little ones planted seeds of courage and heroism in their hearts. The everyday, seemingly unromantic investments I made in my marriage became a rare story of a faithful partnership. It is the unseen actions that shape the story we will tell. We all have landmark moments in our lives where God's will is clear; the real work—and the real reward—is having eyes to see God's work in all the normal days.

My challenge in that time was to look for God's fingerprints in my life. I began to realize that God's purpose for me would not begin in five, ten, or twenty years. His purpose had already begun in my life and it took the form of the children, the husband, the community, and the work I had in front of me each day. Instead of looking ahead for some unrealized hope for fulfillment, I began to see each mundane moment as a potential altar of worship before the Lord of the universe. Every meal I cooked, every neighbor that came for tea, every skinned knee I kissed—each was a brick in the foundation of the legacy I wanted to leave.

To begin to see beauty and purpose in your ordinary days begins with a heart that wants to engage with God. If you don't trust that God is working, then your response to difficulties will always be to crumble once your own personal strength runs out. If you continue to focus on the disorder of the chaos, instead of on the Creator who brings order, you will miss the big picture of God's pervasive presence and work in your life.

Paul reflects this sentiment when he exhorts his friends in the church at Philippi, "Do not be anxious about anything, but in every situation, by prayer and petition, with thanksgiving, present your requests to God" (Philippians 4:6, NIV). He prescribes two antidotes for any anxiety about life they might feel: prayer and thanksgiving. Prayer turns our hearts toward the God of peace; thanksgiving turns our spirits to the peace of God.

To pray is to acknowledge God's reality and presence in your life. When we engage with God in prayer we claim the truth that He is working in even the most frustrating and mundane of days, and we ask for his wisdom and power to see his purpose and act upon it. Giving thanks acknowledges that God is at work in your life—it redirects your anxiety away from immediate difficulties and opens your eyes to see what God has done in the past, is doing in the present, and could do in the future in your life. Through prayer and thanksgiving, we claim each ordinary day as significant and purposeful.

As we came to a stoplight on that Thursday, I paused and looked at my sweet daughter. "Joy, this day is like life. You can't control the unexpected things that will come your way, but you can choose to be thankful and to look for God's grace. Let's embrace this day and enjoy each other." We both let out a sigh, and laughed at what a comedy of errors our day had been. We thanked God for the unexpected time we had to talk alone together, ordered our coffees, and went our ways rejoicing. That day taught me that if you wait to own your life until life is orderly, you will never begin.

— STUDY THE BIBLE —

Hear the Word
Psalm 139:1-6

¹ O LORD, You have searched me and known me.
² You know when I sit down and when I rise up;
You understand my thought from afar.
³ You scrutinize my path and my lying down,
And are intimately acquainted with all my ways.
⁴ Even before there is a word on my tongue,
Behold, O LORD, You know it all.
⁵ You have enclosed me behind and before,
And laid Your hand upon me.
⁶ Such knowledge is too wonderful for me;
It is too high, I cannot attain to it.

Do the Word

In this Psalm David considers how God knows him intimately and is present in each moment of every day. Your life is a unique and beautiful story of God's faithfulness. God is present and working in every day of your life. Read the entire Psalm in your own Bible. How do David's reflections on God's sovereignty change your view of your life? If God is present in every moment of your life, what does that mean to you? Do you live in that reality? How would you change your life if you truly lived in the reality of God's presence in every moment?

Own the Word

My Prayer Isaiah 139:23-24 Please God, look deep inside me. See what is there in my thoughts. 24 Show me if I am following any evil way. Lead me in the right way that has always been true.

Hear the Word
Colossians 3:12-17

12 So, as those who have been chosen of God, holy and beloved, put on a heart of compassion, kindness, humility, gentleness and patience; 13 bearing with one another, and forgiving each other, whoever has a complaint against anyone; just as the Lord forgave you, so also should you. 14 Beyond all these things put on love, which is the perfect bond of unity. 15 Let the peace of Christ rule in your hearts, to which indeed you were called in one body; and be thankful. 16 Let the word of Christ richly dwell within you, with all wisdom teaching and admonishing one another with psalms and hymns and spiritual songs, singing with thankfulness in your hearts to God. 17 Whatever you do in word or deed, do all in the name of the Lord Jesus, giving thanks through Him to God the Father.

19

Do the Word

Every action of your life has the ability to bring glory to God. Are there activities that you think God doesn't care about? How would it change your life to think of every uneventful moment and boring activity as bringing glory to God? How can you own your everyday life and uncontrollable circumstances so that "whatever you do in word or deed" you are doing it all to the glory of god?

Own the Word

Bracelet? Remember — and do it for HIS glory
+ necklace?

_____

_____

_____

_____

_____

— MAKE A PLAN —

Your life is a unique story that can bring glory to God. Take some time to think through the unique challenges and gifts in your life. Here are some areas to consider:

- Family: spouse, children, parents, siblings
- Church: service, outreach, small groups, leadership
- Community: job, neighborhood, school, volunteer
- History: personal testimony, God's past faithfulness

- Personal: talents and skills, financial, home, experience, opportunities

What do you think defines your life and makes it distinct? Is it who you are, what you have, or what you do, or what you've done? What unique resources do you have that affect the choices you make about life? What do you consider to be advantages or strengths to your particular story? Are there any areas of challenge that seem impossible at this moment to overcome that you need to put into God's hands?

(The house - the "stuff", the garden - it's all too much. I must get rid of distracted/useless.
LORD please help me to

— Chapter 2 —

Owning Your Priorities and Commitments

Controlling the Chaos

*I choose to believe that there may be a thousand
big moments embedded in this day, waiting to be
discovered like tiny shards of gold ... the daily,
tiny moments of courage and forgiveness and hope
that we grab on to and extend to one another.*

SHAUNA NIEQUIST (*COLD TANGERINES*)

Baking chocolate chip cookies for the first time is a rite of passage in our family. I can remember the first time I helped my youngest son crack eggs, melt butter, and measure out dry ingredients. His little chest puffed with pride as he busied around the kitchen. At one point, I turned around to answer the phone, and in the space of five seconds I heard a click, a whir, a "poof!" and a distressed five-year-old yelp. I turned around to see the kitchen enveloped in a cloud of flour, and my little baker boy with a look of surprise and desperation written in his furrowed eyebrows.

You can imagine my quick response. I dashed over, turned off the mixer, wiped off the flour from Nathan's terror-white face, put the lid on and helped him use the mixer correctly. The natural response to chaos should be to stop it, clean up the effects of chaos, assess and fix the problem, and carry on. However, I think that when we encounter chaos in life, we often do not respond this way. I so often hear women wanting to know how to "find peace in the chaos," rather than taming the chaos itself.

Imagine if, upon discovering the whirling, open blender, I said to my son, "Now, let's just try to create peace in this chaos." If we approach the chaos of our lives this way, we will either try to ignore the reality of it at our own peril, or we will focus only on the chaos and become caught in a life of damage-control. Rather, we need to respond to it realistically, managing it wisely and objectively. The goal is a rich and fruitful life of living for the kingdom despite the reality of chaos. To begin managing the chaos in our lives, we must learn to identify the sources of chaos, isolate the voices that keep us from owning our lives, and learn to build our lives on a good foundation.

Sources of chaos can be different in every person's life. Perhaps you have difficulty drawing boundaries and saying "no," and that creates a life of chaotic attempts to please everyone by responding to their requests and needs. Perhaps you are an uncontrolled spender who finds yourself under pressure because of the fruits of your lack of frugality. Perhaps you are not blessed with the gift of organization and your stuff, records, closet, and life are out of control. Perhaps your calendar controls you, rather than you controlling it. Whatever your sources of chaos, they cannot be managed until you acknowledge their power and presence in your life.

Once you have pinpointed sources of chaos in your life, you can become proactive and strategic in finding ways to manage chaos. Perhaps, as in the case of Nathan and the mixer, this means you must "turn off" the source of chaos for a while to reassess your priorities. Identifying and strategically handling the chaos in your life will enable you to be in control of the chaos rather than letting the chaos of your life control you. Sometimes it may be as simple as separating yourself from the source of chaos long enough to make a new plan.

Often the chaos around us is not caused by uncontrollable circumstances, but by the incessant and confusing voices that call us in a thousand different directions. With all of the voices of media, friends, family, and church, we can become paralyzed in our good intentions to own our lives. The sheer volume of voices telling us how we ought to live or who we ought to be can become a chaos in itself. I have often said that in the absence of biblical convictions even good people will go the way of culture. To truly own your life, you must identify the voices and messages that you are allowing to let shape your thoughts and emotions, and influence your life. Before we can own our lives, we must learn to let God and his Word be the voice we listen to most closely.

Part of owning life is living life, and life is inevitably messy once in a while. Many years I ago, I reconciled myself to the fact that life will always be full of storms, ear-infected children, and flat tires. However, I also learned that the ability to handle the unexpected waves of life boils down to having a solid foundation from which to engage with life. Jesus speaks about building our lives on the rock of His words (Matthew 7:24-27). To own our lives then means that not only do we manage chaos, but we develop and live out of strong biblical foundations. To stay strong in the storms of life, we must have a life founded securely on the rock of biblical truth.

— STUDY THE BIBLE —

Hear the Word
1 Corinthians 14:33,40

33 ... for God is not a God of confusion but of peace, as in all the churches of the saints. ... 40 But all things must be done properly and in an orderly manner.

Do the Word

In this passage, Paul is instructing the Corinthian church how to stop what had become chaotic worship, and create an orderly and non-chaotic environment in the church. Paul points out that God is a God who, by his very nature, brings order and not chaos. What is the chaos in your life right now that needs God's order? Do you need to manage it, stop it, or get away from it to create a new plan? Where is peace being pushed out of your life by confusion? What can you do to restore a proper sense of order to your life?

Own the Word

❦

Hear the Word
Psalm 34:12-14

12 Who is the man who desires life
And loves length of days that he may see good?
13 Keep you tongue from evil
And your lips from speaking deceit.
14 Depart from evil and do good;
Seek peace and pursue it.

Do the Word

Pursuing peace implies action and intention. Even if you aren't pursuing "evil," what might you be pursuing that is not "good"? What in your life do you need to "depart from" in order to pursue peace? Peace is not just the absence of confusion; it is something we can "seek." In what specific ways are you seeking and pursuing peace in your life right now? How can you be truly intentional about putting away chaos and pursuing peace?

Own the Word

_____

_____

_____

_____

_____

_____

— MAKE A PLAN —

Take some time to consider the sources and kinds of chaos that may be disrupting your life. Here are some potential areas to consider: relationships, health, work overload, inability to say no, messes, finances. What are some strategic ways that you can begin to manage and bring order to this chaos? Do you need to cut off a source of chaos, take a step back and reevaluate, change your reactions, or draw boundaries? Create an action plan to take charge of the chaos in your life.

_____

_____

_____

_____

_____

_____

_____

_____

_____

_____

_____

_____

— Chapter 3 —

Owning Your True Identity
Listening to New Voices

*Define yourself radically as one beloved by God.
This is the true self. Every other identity is
illusion.*

BRENNAN MANNING (*ABBA'S CHILD*)

From a very young age, my youngest daughter Joy never went anywhere without a journal. In her messy and sincere handwriting she chronicled her days, drew pictures, and wrote stories and poems. Sometimes she would climb into my overstuffed chair and read me her entries. To her, life was a story that she had to tell, and as I read the snippets she shared with me I was struck by how enthusiastically and unabashedly she embraced her little stories and memoirs. Her narratives reveled in the innocent acceptance of both God's love and the love of her family.

We are all in the business of telling a story with our lives. However, as we get older, sometimes we let voices other than God's begin to narrate the stories we have to tell. For many years I allowed critical voices from family and friends dictate how I viewed myself and my story. Culture also became a significant voice in my life constantly making me feel ostracized and uncertain of my countercultural decisions. When we begin to weigh others' words more heavily than God's Word, we begin to rehearse narratives about our lives that may not be true. If we are truly to own our lives, we must begin by owning our story and identity spoken to us truly by God.

The secret to owning a new identity is not to try to pretend we are perfect, but to accept our limitations and acknowledge our need for grace. We all have a mixture of personality traits (good and bad), personal wounds, and sinful habits that make us who we are. Throughout my life, I have often found myself relating to Jesus's disciple Peter. Like him, I am very sincere, but my mouth often moves faster than my mind. I try very hard to curb my tongue, and then feel incredibly guilty with another slip-up. It helps me to keep in mind that we live in a fallen world, and try as we might to forget it, we are fallible people; flaws are a part of what it means to be human.

Despite my Peter-like personality and weaknesses, I am confident that God is not surprised by my foibles and imperfections, nor even dissuaded from bothering with me because of my failings. I have long cherished Psalm 103:14, because it reminds me of an important truth that keeps me from giving up: "He Himself knows our frame; He is mindful that we are but dust."

However, beyond simply accepting our limitations, God wants us to delight in who he intends us to be. One of the greatest pleasures of raising my children was observing how uniquely and differently God created each of them. I have two extraverts who live verbally, sing, and bring laughter wherever they go. I also have two introverts who are introspective, insightful, and sensitive. It is my great honor to watch God guide and use them all according to the unique ways he created each of them.

As He did with my children, God takes great care with the creation of every person. From eyelashes and earlobes, to heights and weights, to temperaments and traits, He delights in every human he creates—including you! Learning to accept the special person God has crafted you to be is not prideful; it is an act of faith. When we can accept who we are—the good and the bad, the fun and the foibles, the common and the quirks—then we can be free to deeply thank and worship the One who designed us out of love for a purpose.

The final element of owning our new identity is letting the deep reality of Christ's work shape and transform our lives. Isaiah 1:18 describes the work God will do through Christ: "'Come now, let us settle the matter,' says the LORD. 'Though your sins are like scarlet, they shall be as white as snow.'" Jesus' work on the cross means that all who accept Him as Lord and Savior are redeemed and made clean, "knowing this, that our old self was crucified with [Christ], in order that our body of sin might be done away with, so that we would no longer be slaves to sin" (Romans 6:6). Whatever is in the past stays in the past because when you are "in Christ [you are] a new creature; the old things passed away; behold new things have come" (1 Corinthians 5:17).

We all have many different voices speaking into our lives—spouse, family, friends, church, media, parents, memories. However, too many times the voices we hear speaking to us are our own, narrating opinions and observations that may or may not be true. Paul seems to understand the nature of those voices inside our heads and hearts when he tells the Christians in Corinth, "We are destroying speculations and every lofty thing raised up against the knowledge of God, and *we are taking every thought captive to the obedience of Christ*" (2 Corinthians 10:5, italics mine). He even suggests that wrong thinking can become a "fortress" that needs to be destroyed (see: 10:3-4). Our spiritual battle is take those negative thoughts captive and give them to Christ, so our new and true identity can grow and take charge.

Listening to the voices of others to determine our worth is a pointless task that will end in disappointment. Only God can truly satisfy, and only in Him can we see our real, redeemed selves. In quietness, and strength, we must learn to listen to the voice that truly knows us and loves us, and can tell us who we really are. We are His.

— STUDY THE BIBLE —

Hear the Word
Psalm 107:1-2

¹ Oh give thanks to the LORD, for He is good, for His lovingkindness is everlasting. ² Let the redeemed of the LORD say so, whom He has redeemed from the hand of the adversary.

Do the Word

Psalm 107 commands its readers to tell the story of God's work in their lives. So often we forget the beautiful and life-empowering story of God's work in our lives. Why do you think it is so important to remember the story of God's faithfulness? Sometimes when we listen to the voices of the world, we forget the power, love, and forgiveness God has spoken over our life. Do you ever find yourself forgetting God's voice and story in your life? What can you do to reclaim His story for you?

Own the Word

_____

_____

_____

_____

_____

_____

Hear the Word
Romans 8:37-39

37 But in all these things we overwhelmingly conquer through Him who loved us. 38 For I am convinced that neither death, nor life, nor angels, nor principalities, nor things present, nor things to come, nor powers, 39 nor height, nor depth, nor any other created thing, will be able to separate us from the love of God, which is in Christ Jesus our Lord.

Do the Word

In this beautiful passage of encouragement, Paul intends to impress upon the Roman church that God's love for them is unchangeable and powerful. Let this reality sink into your own heart. Have you ever truly accepted that God's love for you is not conditional upon your prior righteousness and that He will never stop loving you? How does knowing the depth of God's love for you affect your responses to difficulties and challenges?

Own the Word

_____

_____

_____

_____

_____

_____

❧

Hear the Word
2 Corinthians 5:16-17

16 Therefore from now on we recognize no one according to the flesh; even though we have known Christ according to the flesh, yet now we know Him in this way no longer. 17 Therefore if anyone is in Christ, he is a new creature; the old things passed away; behold, new things have come.

Do the Word

What does it mean that "in Christ" you are a "new creature"? As you have come to know and grow in Christ,
what "old things [have] passed away"? What "new things
have come"? If you really started believing, every day,
that you are a new creature in Christ, what difference
would it make in your life? Take some time to journal
and articulate what this means for your life, self-
perception, past, and relationships.

Own the Word

_____

_____

_____

_____

_____

_____

— MAKE A PLAN —

What voices might be causing you to live in a way that is
not consistent with what God says is true about who you
are in Christ? How are you "taking every thought captive" to make sure you are strengthening your new and
true identity? Journal or discuss with a friend the questions below about the voices you hear.

- Others' voices: Are there people in your life who have spoken negative narratives about you that you have believed and lived by? Identify the narratives and write them out. Are they consistent with God's attitude toward you? If not, how can you change them?
- Cultural voices: Culture chimes a cacophony of voices telling you how you should think, look, live, and love. Do you let these voices govern your life? Why?
- Personal voices: Do you practice telling yourself a negative story of your life? Do you constantly speak negative things about yourself? What can you do to change that narrative to one that reflects God's view of your identity in Christ?

_____

_____

_____

_____

_____

_____

_____

_____

_____

_____

_____

— Chapter 4 —

Owning Your Life Vision
Living with the End in Mind

You've gotta dance like there's nobody watching,
Love like you'll never be hurt,
Sing like there's nobody listening,
And live like it's heaven on earth.

WILLIAM W. PURKEY

G iving gifts to my children is a special delight for me. One Christmas after a great deal of consideration, careful selection, and a healthy amount of sneaking, Clay and I were elated with the gift we had picked out for our precious son Joel: his first guitar.

It was a perfect fit for our most musical child. At only eighteen months old, Joel was singing "Twinkle, Twinkle, Little Star" perfectly and on pitch, and he began harmonizing at age three. As he grew, we watched his abilities blossom, so a guitar was an obvious choice to help him hone his gifts. That morning, pajama-clad and holding hot chocolate, Clay and I smiled as we watched Joel open the guitar case in wonder. Seeing the look on his face as he ran his hands over the smooth shiny body of his new musical tool confirmed our choice of a gift.

Twelve years later, I sat with tears in my eyes, clapping with all my mama-heart as Joel walked across the stage at his Berklee College of Music graduation. The in-between years had been filled with picking, plucking, and strumming that built up calluses on his fingers to be able to fret the strings more easily. And along with the guitar would come new instruments to learn, new skills, and many hours of "jamming" in our living room. The little boy who had once relished his first real instrument in my living room now stood before me on stage, Summa Cum Laude graduate and Composer of the Year, and an emerging master of his trade.

Being a parent has so often given me a deeper understanding of God's feelings towards me. My delight in giving gifts to my children recalls to mind what Jesus said in the sermon on the mount: "If you then, being evil, know how to give good gifts to your children, how much more will your Father who is in heaven give what is good to those who ask Him!" (Matthew 7:11). The true delight of my parent's heart was not only giving Joel the gift but watching his grateful and faithful response.

Imagine if we had given Joel the guitar, and he had thanked us for it, but then over the years it sat in a corner of his room gathering dust. We did not give him the guitar with a contract that said, "You must practice with this, be faithful, and become a skilled musician." We gave it to him freely. But his faithfulness delighted our hearts as he put the gift to good use. Just as Clay and I knew our son and gave him a gift that we knew would both delight and empower him, so God gives to us even more generously since he is the one who knit us together "in the womb" creating and weaving into our being the very fabric of our personalities and personhood.

The test of our legacy is how we choose to engage with the gifts of life God has given us. He trusts us with a story, a personality, a family, resources, skills, and even heartaches. When we engage and respond to his grace, it delights God's heart. He gives grace unconditionally, but there is a way in which His gifts in our lives are incomplete unless we choose to accept them with thankfulness and use them to His glory. With each time we practice faithfulness, we weave a bit more color and thread into the fabric of our legacy.

Living with the end in mind means living with an attitude that says, "What has God given me with which to be faithful today? How can I invest in His kingdom, even in this seemingly mundane moment?" And sometimes faithfulness is *very* mundane.

I remember in my first days of working in communist Eastern Europe finding myself wondering if my life really was making a difference for the kingdom. I had imagined an Acts of the Apostles-worthy picture of myself boldly proclaiming the gospel from rooftops and bringing thousands to Christ. However, when I arrived, I found myself spending long days pouring over language textbooks, many hours simply learning how to live in a new and very foreign culture, and daily putting my broken Polish to use in an attempt to find food and supplies. In that period of my life, faithfulness meant being thankful, persevering with the language, and looking for the Lord's work in my seemingly insignificant days.

God always blesses small efforts of faithfulness. Throughout my life I have learned to love the verse which says, "Do not despise these small beginnings, for the LORD rejoices to see the work begin" (Zechariah 4:10, NLT). In those days of seeing the work begin, I took God at His word that my small life would count for something. I trusted that the kingdom would thrive in my life like a tiny mustard seed that grew into strong branches for the birds to rest in (Mark 4:31).

Recently, I was visited by a dear friend whom I had led to the Lord during my time in Poland. Sharing tea with her, I saw how those small seeds of faithfulness had grown over the years. Long after I left Poland, this woman went on with her husband to become the leader of outreaches in multiple countries in Eastern Europe. The small seed of my faithful witness had grown into a strong tree, and now I smile with thankfulness as I ponder it.

God never wastes faithfulness. Whether it be in learning to play the guitar, living a faithful life in a foreign land, or anything else that requires deep dedication, our Lord takes our little and makes it into much. Imagine what God might have in store with which to bless your faithfulness.

— STUDY THE BIBLE —

Hear the Word
Psalm 90:10-12

10 As for the days of our life, they contain seventy years, or if due to strength, eighty years, yet their pride is but labor and sorrow; for soon it is gone and we fly away. 11 Who understand the power of Your anger and your fury, according to the fear that is due You? 12 So teach us to number our days, that we may present to You a heart of wisdom.

Do the Word

In this passage, in the only psalm attributed to Moses, the writer contemplates the brevity and difficulty of life, and the importance of living a life of faithfulness for God. Ask God to help you to see the significance of your life, even though it is a brief time before "we fly away." How can you "number [your] days"? What does God need to "teach" you so you can do that effectively? How will numbering your days help you develop a "heart of wisdom"? What will it mean for you to live faithfully and wisely, with the end in mind?

Own the Word

_____

_____

_____

_____

_____

_____

❧

Hear the Word
Galatians 6:7-10

7 Do not be deceived, God is not mocked; for whatever a man sows, this he will also reap. 8 For the one who sows to his own flesh will from the flesh reap corruption, but the one who sows to the Spirit will from the Spirit reap eternal life. ⁹ *Let us not lose heart in doing good, for in due time we will reap if we do not grow weary.* ¹⁰ *So then, while we have opportunity, let us do good to all people, and especially to those who are of the household of the faith.*

Do the Word

In this exhausting world, it is easy to become weary and give in to compromise. It was the same in Paul's day, and why he exhorted the Galatians to not grown weary of doing good. Are you becoming weary of doing good? Being faithful in an unfaithful world can be wearying! Journal, or talk with a friend about some of these questions. What good are you growing weary of doing? What seeds of faithfulness, love, and humility are you planting now?

Own the Word

_____

_____

_____

_____

_____

_____

— MAKE A PLAN —

Take an inventory of your life. In what areas is God asking you to remain faithful? Look back on the list in

Chapter 1 and write down a plan about how you can do that well. What can you do to make sure you are building a legacy of faith in each of those areas?

- Family: spouse, children, parents, siblings
- Church: service, outreach, small groups, leadership
- Community: job, neighborhood, school, volunteer
- History: personal testimony, God's past faithfulness
- Personal: talents and skills, financial, home, experience, opportunities

_____

_____

_____

_____

_____

_____

_____

_____

_____

_____

_____

_____

_____

— Chapter 5 —

Owning God's Training

Looking to God as Your Life Coach

You are braver than you believe, stronger than
you seem, and smarter than you think.

A.A. MILNE

*E*ven the birds aren't awake yet, I thought to myself.
As I slipped from the pool's edge into the water, I shivered from the chill. I took a deep breath and bobbed my capped head under the heavily chlorinated water. As an asthmatic, many sports were hard for me, but I excelled at swimming because I could control my breath. A shrill whistle sung out and echoed throughout the hard walls of the gym as I shot myself off under water from the pool wall to begin a swim practice that, while rendering me exhausted, would fill me with exhilaration and strength.

I spent many days swimming as a young adult. Swimming did not come naturally to me; it was a skill hard won with hard work. I spent hundreds of hours practicing, many weekends at swim meets, and during one summer my hair was very nearly green from the chemicals in the water. Whenever I would become exasperated with myself, my coach would encourage and challenge me to keep on going, helping me to adjust my method so I could be an effective swimmer. Even now at sixty-one years young, although I do not have as much opportunity to swim, I love the chance to dip my head under the water and shoot off the wall again just as I did when I was a lanky teenager. Though my muscles are weaker than they once were, swimming is a skill that has never left me.

Swimming taught me to see God as my coach in the midst of life's trials. Paul says in 1 Corinthians 9:24, "Do you not know that those who run in a race all run, but only one receives the prize? Run in such a way that you may win." As we live by faith, we are under the guidance of the Holy Spirit training and instructing us how to live a righteousness life. When we see our days as a part of God's training for righteousness, it strengthens us to not compromise.

In my race of life, there have been so many times where my spiritual muscles felt exhausted, my heart was sore, and I didn't think I could hang on for another lap of life. There were some mornings when I would wake up and pray, "Lord, I don't know if I can practice righteousness today, I'm so exhausted." Throughout the years, I began to see those times as significant and fruitful. I can see now that those seasons helped strengthen my spiritual muscles. Like a good coach, God was always present and urged me on to do better. "I know you're tired, but I am with you, I love you, and I have a plan for your life. I have overcome, and I want to help you overcome; you need only live in that truth. I'm here. I will help you."

God's goal for working in my life is always to help me build stronger spiritual muscles; I cannot grow stronger on my own. John 14:26 says: "But the Helper, the Holy Spirit, whom the Father will send in My name, He will teach you all things, and bring to your remembrance all that I said to you." In all of our trials, God is with us, training us and encouraging us to stretch the spiritual muscles He has given us. We do not have to face trials alone. God is always with us to comfort and guide us, even when we are unable to feel it.

God loves you. This simple truth is one of the most easily forgotten or misconstrued. It is easy, when encountering difficulties, to go to dark places in our minds, thinking maybe God is disappointed with us. However, the scriptural representation of God heartily contradicts this idea. Hebrews 4:15 shows us that God's attitude toward us is one of sacrificial love and deep understanding of our need for Him. It says: "For we do not have a high priest who cannot sympathize with our weaknesses, but One who has been tempted in all things as we are, yet without sin." When you pray, do so with the confidence that God loves you and understands every trial you encounter.

Finally, it is vital to bear in mind that God's plan reaches far beyond what we can see. As we grow in our walk with God, we are gradually moving toward a destiny of glory that we cannot even comprehend yet. Second Peter 3:13 gives us a glimpse of this: "But according to His promise we are looking for new heavens and a new earth, in which righteousness dwells." As we practice righteousness, living in response to God's grace, we live in anticipation of God's eventual renewal of all things through his kingdom.

God is with us for the long haul. As we choose to engage, rather than withdraw, we allow Him to strengthen our spiritual muscles so that we can "run in a way so as to win." If I had forgone every swim practice when I was tired or sore, I would not have developed the skill I so delight in even today. In the same way, if we withdraw from difficulties in life, rather than looking to our redeeming life coach, we cannot know what peaceful fruit of righteousness (Hebrews 12:11) God may be waiting patiently to bestow upon us.

— STUDY THE BIBLE —

Hear the Word
Hebrews 12:1-3, 9-11

12 Therefore, since we have so great a cloud of witnesses surrounding us, let us also lay aside every encumbrance and the sin which so easily entangles us, and let us run with endurance the race that is set before us, 2 fixing our eyes on Jesus, the author and perfecter of faith, who for the joy set before Him endured the cross, despising the shame, and has sat down at the right hand of the throne of God. 3 For consider Him who has endured such hostility by sinners against Himself, so that you will not grow weary and lose heart. ... 9 Furthermore, we had earthly fathers to discipline us, and we respected them; shall we not much rather be subject to the Father of spirits, and live? 10 For they disciplined us for a short time as seemed best to them, but He disciplines us for our good, so that we may share His holiness. 11 All discipline for the moment seems not to be joyful, but sorrowful; yet to those who have been trained by it, afterwards it yields the peaceful fruit of righteousness.

Do the Word

In this familiar passage, the author exhorts the reader to look at life as a race to be won in the power of God. We can look to the "great ... cloud of witnesses" the author has just described in the previous chapter to keep us going when we encounter difficulties. As athletes in a race of faith, their examples remind us that we can overcome "every encumbrance" just as they did with God's help. We are encouraged to "[fix] our eyes on Jesus" to help us "run with endurance" our own race, just as He ran His. And we are to understand that God, our Father, "disciplines us for our good" so that we can "share in His holiness" and also reap "the peaceful fruit of righteousness." Do you look at your life this way? How does it impact your life to think of Jesus as your model, and of God as a Father who is training you to be a powerful athlete for his kingdom?

Own the Word

Hear the Word
Matthew 25:14-18, 29-30

14 "For it is just like a man about to go on a journey, who called his own slaves and entrusted his possessions to them. 15 To one he gave five talents, to another, two, and to another, one, each according to his own ability; and he went on his journey. 16 Immediately the one who had received the five talents went and traded with them, and gained five more talents. 17 In the same manner the one who had received the two talents gained two more. 18 But he who received the one talent went away, and dug a hole in the ground and hid his master's money. ...

29 "For to everyone who has, more shall be given, and he will have an abundance; but from the one who does not have, even what he does have shall be taken away. 30 Throw out the worthless slave into the outer darkness; in that place there will be weeping and gnashing of teeth.

Do the Word

Read the full version of this familiar parable again in your own Bible. God has entrusted you with talents—a story, abilities, circumstances, a special place in the world, the gospel of the kingdom. He is asking you to be a good steward, or manger, of all that he has given to you. What does it look like for you to make good use of the particular resources He has entrusted to you for your time on earth? It doesn't matter how many "talents" you have received from God, but only what you do with the talents you've been given. How are you investing the talents God has given to you for His kingdom? How are you seeing your talents grow for God? What can you do to increase your faithfulness and stewardship of what God has invested in you?

Own the Word

_____

_____

_____

_____

_____

_____

— MAKE A PLAN —

We all have some aspects of our lives that are more difficult for us than the other less-challenging parts of our lives. In what areas of life do you need training to become stronger to overcome difficulties and weaknesses? God is not a condemning divine drillmaster waiting for you to try harder, but a loving father who can't wait to help you grow. There are many things you can do to pursue the goal of strengthening weak areas:

- Ask the Holy Spirit to reveal weak areas of your life in which you could grow and become stronger.
- Begin keeping a prayer journal of specific requests about the areas the Spirit shows you.
- Begin jotting down Bible verses that you encounter that encourage and strengthen your faith.
- Find a friend who can encourage and pray with you, and help you grow in the areas you are praying about.

Identify one area of weakness in your life that you can work on, and what you plan to do.

_____

_____

_____

_____

_____

_____

_____

_____

_____

_____

_____

— Chapter 6 —

Owning the Mystery of His Supremacy

Resting in the Transcendence of God

As long as you are looking down, you cannot see something that is above you.

C.S. LEWIS

The world of a young child is full of wonder and trust. When we lived on my mother-in-law's farmland in Texas, I remember taking my daughter Joy out for a walk on the land. She was two and walked with wobbly confidence as I held her hand, ready to catch her at any moment her inexperienced limbs betrayed her. It was a world of firsts. She marveled in joyous raptures at the Monarch butterfly that fluttered by us. She giggled as I blew on the dandelion in her hand, the fluffy seeds floating daintily in the wind. As we made our way back home, she grew tired from walking so I scooped her up in my arms. She melted into my shoulder in sleepy abandon.

I believe this is a small image of how God wants us to be with Him. In childhood we encounter the world in terms of trust and wonder, but as we grow we learn what it means to worry and doubt. Where we once saw the innumerable stars, we begin to see the seemingly innumerable bills. Where we once laughed at the soft wriggling body of a puppy, we now cry at the hurtful words of people whose approval we desperately wish we could win. The love of God was something we once rested in, and now we doubt when trials come our way.

It seems to me that the worries of adulthood make our vision smaller. Instead of seeing the vast beauty of the world that God has made and the extravagant love with which He loves us, we narrow our vision to the small frame of temporary trials. This is not to say that our trials are not difficult or painful, but that in our forgetfulness of God's transcendence we fail to see the grace that supports us all around. When we lose this greater vision, we do not walk as "more than conquerors" (Romans 8:37, NIV), but as though suspicious and afraid of the world.

The truth is that God's power is greater than we can imagine, and his sustaining grace for our lives is deeper than we can ever understand. Psalm 8:3-4 says, "When I consider Your heavens, the work of your fingers, the moon and the stars, which You have ordained; what is man that You take thought of him, and the son of man that You care for him?" This Psalm declares the truth that the God who threw the stars into place is the God who cares for us. God's care for us is present and personal, but it also reaches into a beautiful future we can't even see.

In 1 Corinthians 2:9, Paul encourages young Christians, reminding them of all the "Things which eye has not seen and ear has not heard, and which have not entered the heart of man, all that God has prepared for those who love Him." As Joy once did with me, we can walk hand-in-hand with God, trusting His power and love to see us through every day of our lives.

However, while we can understand something intellectually, we need to practice dwelling on this truth so it will begin to permeate the thoughts of our hearts. If I am to trust in the transcendence of God, I must practice looking up to see His work. As sinful and fallible humans, trust and wonder is not our predisposition. Becoming like a child, as Jesus commands us to do, requires a retraining of our heart habits.

One way I do this is by meditating on how God is already at work in my life. This requires stillness of my spirit. Often, I rise before my children awaken, light a candle, and brew a cup of coffee. In that quiet moment, I breathe out the troubles of my heart, resting peacefully in my Father who knows and understands everything I'm thinking and feeling. As I breathe His presence and peace back into my heart, I contemplate how even this breath is a grace. I write down the things for which I am thankful, and how I can already see God's hands at work in my life. Finally, I read a bit of God's Word, asking the Lord to write the truth of His faithfulness on my heart.

Just as I delighted in carrying my sleepy Joy in my arms, God delights in providing for, loving, and carrying us. Practicing orienting my heart towards trust and worship enables me to catch a small glimpse of His glorious power and love. Resting in His transcendence helps me to open my eyes to the gift of beauty He is waiting to bestow upon me. Instead of seeing only the small frame of my worries and trials, I can begin to see all of life in the context of the beautiful story God is writing.

— STUDY THE BIBLE —

Hear the Word
Psalm 8

¹ *O LORD, our Lord,*
How majestic is Your name in all the earth,
Who have displayed Your splendor above the heavens!
² *From the mouth of infants and nursing babes You have*
established strength
Because of Your adversaries,
To make the enemy and the revengeful cease.
³ *When I consider Your heavens, the work of Your fingers,*
The moon and the stars, which You have ordained;
⁴ *What is man that You take thought of him,*
And the son of man that You care for him?
⁵ *Yet You have made him a little lower than God,*
And You crown him with glory and majesty!
⁶ *You make him to rule over the works of Your hands;*
You have put all things under his feet,
⁷ *All sheep and oxen,*
And also the beasts of the field,
⁸ *The birds of the heavens and the fish of the sea,*
Whatever passes through the paths of the seas.
⁹ *O LORD, our Lord,*
How majestic is Your name in all the earth!

Do the Word

Isn't it amazing that the God who cares for the vast magnificence of the universe cares for your personal needs and concerns? When, like the Psalmist, we look to the heavens, our troubles become smaller. When you "consider" and ponder on all that God has created, how does it change your thoughts about Him? How does it change your perspective to dwell on the greatness of God and beauty of His creation? Worshiping God for His power and glory helps us be drawn away from the petty and painful things in our life.

Own the Word

_____

_____

_____

_____

_____

_____

❦

Hear the Word
Job 38:1-7

¹ Then the LORD answered Job out of the whirlwind and said,² "Who is this that darkens counsel
By words without knowledge?
³ "Now gird up your loins like a man,
And I will ask you, and you instruct Me!
⁴ "Where were you when I laid the foundation of the earth?
Tell Me, if you have understanding,
⁵ Who set its measurements? Since you know.
Or who stretched the line on it?
⁶ "On what were its bases sunk?
Or who laid its cornerstone,
⁷ When the morning stars sang together
And all the sons of God shouted for joy?

Do the Word

When Job encountered incredible pain and confusion, God's response was to point him to creation to tell him of His magnificence. power, and glory. Why do you think God did this? Why is this what Job needed to hear? Read this passage (and all of chapters 38-41 in your own Bible) as though God is speaking it to you in a time of trial and trouble. How does it strike your spirit?

Own the Word

_____

_____

_____

_____

_____

_____

— MAKE A PLAN —

Intentionally carve out some time to go somewhere beautiful in nature, a place that moves your spirit with the grandeur of God. Open your heart to worship God for his creativity and beauty of the world He has made. Take a journal and write down your thoughts. How can you be more resolute in your trust in God? How does the beauty and vastness of God's creation affect you?

— Chapter 7 —

Owning the Holy Spirit's Strength through You

Allowing God's Spirit to Breathe in You

Trying to do the Lord's work in your own strength is the most confusing, exhausting, and tedious of all work. But when you are filled with the Holy Spirit, then the ministry of Jesus just flows out of you.

CORRIE TEN BOOM

It's a miracle! I thought to myself as I closed the door behind me. Somehow I had managed to slip out of bed without waking Clay, slip on my shoes and a comforting sweater, and get out the door for a Saturday morning coffee. As I sat in the cozy corner of the café, coffee in hand, I basked in the delight of a stolen moment alone. I read my morning verses, and jotted down some deep thoughts in my journal. *I will be so kind, very loving, and patient today,* I thought. And then my phone rang.

"Mom! Where are you? What are we going to do today?" I responded patiently with this child (how could I not be patient in such a lovely moment?) and explained that I'd be home in just a little while to do something fun with the whole clan. Even just thirty minutes alone was rejuvenating for me, but I sighed nonetheless.

But then the phone rang again.

"Hey, honey! Who's going to take Joy downtown for her appointment?" This time it was my husband's voice. I pondered on this. There were no less than four adults in our home who could drive; perhaps one of them could manage? This was my one morning alone. Even so, I continued to talk with Clay as we puzzle-pieced schedules. As I ended the phone call, I breathed deeply. The coffee and quiet started to enchant my soul back into a pleasant attitude.

And then the phone rang. Again.

Everyone was hungry and wanted breakfast. With another sigh, I gathered myself, thanked God for the few moments of peace, and resolved to enjoy the day and cherish my beloved ones. This thought was barely a notion in my mind when I walked through the door to discover the dog had thrown up on the new carpet.

I think I need another cup of coffee.

So many times in my life I have encountered the tension between wanting to be Spirit-filled and gracious, and then being overwhelmed by my own attitudes, the unexpected situations of my life, or the many clashing personalities of my family members. Life tends to have a sandpaper effect on my attempts to be holy. These times have led me explore what it means to live in the power of the Spirit.

Throughout Scripture, the Holy Spirit is often described using the analogy of wind, or breath. When explaining the mysteries of the Spirit to Nicodemus, Jesus said: "The wind blows where it wishes and you hear the sound of it, but do not know where it comes from and where it is going; so is everyone who is born of the Spirit" (John 3:8). The Greek word Jesus uses is *pnuema*, which can be translated as wind, breath, or spirit. Later, when Jesus is commissioning his disciples, Scripture manifests the metaphor into an actual happenstance: "And when He had said this, He breathed on them and said to them, 'Receive the Holy Spirit'" (John 20:22). Again and again the Holy Spirit is described as breath which brings life, and wind which provides direction.

Breath is a daily necessity. We cannot live without breathing, and it is a constant need moment to moment. The same sort of dependence we have on breathing is how we ought to depend on the Holy Spirit. Living in the power of the Holy Spirit means letting the Spirit of God be the breath that allows me to make it through every day. Relying on the assistance of the Holy Spirit should become as natural to me as breathing in and out.

When our bodies run out of oxygen, they quickly begin to function poorly and eventually die. In the same way, if we try to survive only on the occasional breath of the Spirit, we will spiritually suffocate. Sometimes, we cut off our spiritual oxygen by feeling guilty for failing to fall into that rhythm of the Spirit. Instead of experiencing guilt, we should instead quickly breathe in, praying, "Lord, I need you. Fill me and direct me."

Living in the Holy Spirit also means being attentive to the wind of the Spirit that directs our lives. Learning to be directed by the Spirit is a mysterious dance—things change quickly, and simply following the rules won't allow us to stay light on our feet. Instead, it requires us to trust our partner, living in attentiveness and expectancy.

As you pray and read Scripture, open your heart and ponder what it means to act in obedience to what you have received from the Holy Spirit. Acknowledge to yourself and to God that the Holy Spirit is already at work in your life, and pray for the wisdom and strength to see it and act upon it.

As in my moment at the coffee shop, I had to sway with the movement of the Spirit in my life. Circumstances change, but the Spirit of God is a trustworthy dance partner. I must constantly breath in the Spirit if I am to live a robust Christian life.

— STUDY THE BIBLE —

Hear the Word
Acts 1:5-8

1 The first account I composed, Theophilus, about all that Jesus began to do and teach, 2 until the day when He was taken up to heaven, after He had by the Holy Spirit given orders to the apostles whom He had chosen. 3 To these He also presented Himself alive after His suffering, by many convincing proofs, appearing to them over a period of forty days and speaking of the things concerning the kingdom of God. 4 Gathering them together, He commanded them not to leave Jerusalem, but to wait for what the Father had promised, "Which," He said, "you heard of from Me; 5 for John baptized with water, but you will be baptized with the Holy Spirit not many days from now." 6 So when they had come together, they were asking Him, saying, "Lord, is it at this time You are restoring the kingdom to Israel?" 7 He said to them, "It is not for you to know times or epochs which the Father has fixed by His own authority; 8 but you will receive power when the Holy Spirit has come upon you; and you shall be My witnesses both in Jerusalem, and in all Judea and Samaria, and even to the remotest part of the earth."

Do the Word

In your own Bible, scan through chapters 1-10 in the book of Acts, the account of the beginning of the church. As you do, highlight each time the Holy Spirit is mentioned. When the Holy Spirit works, what happens? In what ways does the early church experience the Holy Spirit, whether individuals or the gathered body? Note how often the Holy Spirit works in very practical and ordinary ways, and in extraordinary ways.

Own the Word

_____

_____

_____

_____

_____

_____

❦

Hear the Word
Galatians 5:22-25

[22] But the fruit of the Spirit is love, joy, peace, patience, kindness, goodness, faithfulness, [23] gentleness, self-control; against such things there is no law. [24] Now those who belong to Christ Jesus have crucified the flesh with its passions and desires. [25] If we live by the Spirit, let us also walk by the Spirit.

Do the Word

Take some time to read this passage several times. Thoughtfully consider each fruit of the Spirit. Which fruits of the Spirit are most evident in your life? In what areas do you see growth potential? Think of this passage like an inventory of the fruits of the Holy Spirit in your own life. Is there a specific fruit of the Spirit you feel God is calling you to grow in? Is there one that you are strong in that you need to use more in your life? What does it mean that you "belong to Christ" and that you "live by the Spirit"? What then does it mean when Paul exhorts that we are to "walk by the Spirit"?

Own the Word

_____

_____

_____

_____

_____

_____

— MAKE A PLAN —

Consider your inventory of the fruits of the Holy Spirit and pick one. As you read Scripture, begin to write down verses that speak to you about the particular "fruit" you picked. Take a few moments every day to invite the Holy

Spirit to speak to you, fill you, and help you grow in the area you chose. Repeat this pattern each day, and jot down your thoughts on how you see the Holy Spirit teaching and filling you as you "walk by the Spirit" along the way.

_____

_____

_____

_____

_____

_____

_____

_____

_____

_____

— Chapter 8 —

Owning the Spiritual Disciplines

Cultivating the Practices That Deepen Your Faith

*The more we know Him, the more we will desire
to know Him. As love increases with knowledge,
the more we know God, the more we will truly
love Him. We will learn to love Him equally in
times of distress or in times of great joy.*

BROTHER LAWRENCE

"Well, I don't know, it's just, like..." These words
had barely slipped out of Joy's mouth before my
eyebrows raised at her and we both started laughing. Ever since she had returned during breaks from her university in Southern California, the word "like" frequently visited itself upon her vocabulary. Joy had never been a
"like" girl before, but after a few months in the land of
surfboards and juice shops, that word, along with the
slow rhythm of the Southern California accent, had begun to work itself into her way of speaking.

"I don't mean to, Mom! It's just the way I hear all of
the voices around me speaking, and I can't help but let it
slip in to the way I speak and think."

I believe that Joy's "like" predicament exhibits the
power of the voices to which we listen. We live in a cul-

ture that loves to quote movies, books, and song lyrics. I marvel as I watch my kids hold almost entire conversations in quotes from their favorite characters from television and literature. I have realized that as my children engage in certain forms of media, those forms begin to shape their vocabulary and way of thinking.

The same is true of friend groups. I am amused to see best friends who inadvertently dress and speak like each other, or friend groups who all order similar coffee concoctions. It is a part of human nature that we naturally begin to emulate who or what we spend time with and on, respectively. Proverbs says, "He who walks with wise men will be wise, but the companion of fools will suffer harm" (Proverbs 13:20). We are formed by the voices that we allow to speak into our lives.

This is why spiritual disciplines are important. Cultivating such practices in your life creates a space in which one can be formed by the voice of God. In reading Scripture, we allow God's truth to speak to our heart. In prayer, we listen for the whisper of the Holy Spirit. In honoring the Sabbath and resting, we train our hearts to rest in the knowledge that God will always provide. Spiritual disciplines remove distractions from our practice of faith, allowing the voice of God in our spirit to shape our vocabulary and our attitudes.

Women often say to me, "I'm too busy to have a quiet time or pray" or "I have young children and don't ever seem to have free time" or "I don't want to be legalistic about it." When I hear this, I often respond with a question: "What voices are you allowing to shape your view of the world instead of Scripture and the Holy Spirit?" We are all in the business of listening to voices, and allowing various channels to broadcast over the rest.

I often find that when I don't think I have time to listen to God, it is because I am busy prioritizing other voices. This is something that happens to the best of us. For some that may be wasting time on social media, putting an overemphasis on perfect housekeeping, or getting caught in an endless cycle of busyness. Of course, there is nothing inherently wrong about social media, housekeeping, and a busy schedule. None of those things is necessarily bad, but nothing can replace the voice of God, and the value gained from time in His presence.

The spiritual disciplines are not about legalism, but about developing practices which tune your ear to the truth of Scripture, your will to the practice of faithfulness, and your heart to communion with God. My children are able to bring to mind the quotes of many of their favorite literary characters because of the time they have spent invested in reading. In the same way, as you invest time in Scripture, the Holy Spirit will begin to bring passages to your mind when you encounter difficult situations.

As you read and let the truth of Scripture sink into your heart, it will begin to shape your vocabulary and thoughts about the world. When truth is in your patterns of thinking, it will alter the way you respond to situations in your life.

At the heart of any spiritual discipline is relationship with God. Genesis 3:8 says, "They heard the sound of the LORD God walking in the garden in the cool of the day, and the man and his wife hid themselves from the presence of the LORD God among the trees of the garden." From the very beginning, God desired that we might share an intimate relationship with Him. His intention was that we would delight in our relationship with Him and reflect his image in us. Though the fall broke that relationship, Christ made a way for us to be once again in communion with God. God's desire to be in relationship with us is the same as it was in Eden. Spiritual disciplines do not take the place of that relationship, but rather, through the Holy Spirit, they give our impatient and sinful souls a way to engage with God. Because God delights in our relationship, He will always bless a heart that seeks to engage with Him.

— STUDY THE BIBLE —

Hear the Word
Psalm 119:9-16

9 How can a young man keep his way pure?
By keeping it according to Your word.
10 With all my heart I have sought You;
Do not let me wander from Your commandments.
11 Your word I have treasured in my heart,
That I may not sin against You.
12 Blessed are You, O LORD;
Teach me Your statutes.
13 With my lips I have told of
All the ordinances of Your mouth.
14 I have rejoiced in the way of Your testimonies,
As much as in all riches.
15 I will meditate on Your precepts
And regard Your ways.
16 I shall delight in Your statutes;
I shall not forget Your word.

Do the Word

Psalm 119, the longest in the psalter at 176 verses, is devoted to teaching about and celebrating the role of Scripture in the life of the one who follows God. David speaks of dwelling on God's words even when he is in bed. God's Holy Scripture is one of the main ways we can interact with Him. Why do think God places such importance on Scripture? Do you place a high value on God's Word in your life? What ways do you "treasure" the Word of God in your heart? How do you "delight" in His Word? What are doing to "not forget" God's Word?

Own the Word

_____

_____

_____

_____

_____

_____

❧

Hear the Word
Acts 2:42-47

42 They were continually devoting themselves to the apostles' teaching and to fellowship, to the breaking of bread and to prayer. 43 Everyone kept feeling a sense of awe; and many wonders and signs were taking place through the apostles. ⁴⁴ And all those who had believed were together and had all things in common; ⁴⁵ and they began selling their property and possessions and were sharing them with all, as anyone might have need.⁴⁶ Day by day continuing with one mind in the temple, and breaking bread from house to house, they were taking their meals together with gladness and sincerity of heart, ⁴⁷ praising God and having favor with all the people. And the Lord was adding to their number day by day those who were being saved. ¹⁶ I shall delight in Your statutes; I shall not forget Your word.

Do the Word

Almost the first thing the new believers of the early church did upon receiving the gospel was to implement spiritual practices to nurture faith (fellowship, teaching of the apostles, breaking of bread, and prayer). This was no lifeless liturgy, but rather a way of keeping the teachings of Christ alive. Why do you think this was the church's first response? Do you take these sorts of practices seriously in your life? What is the practice you most neglect? What is the practice you most pursue?

Own the Word

— MAKE A PLAN —

Like any relationship, pursuing God requires intentionality and time. Investing time in the Word, prayer, solitude, and other practices to deepen your faith requires a plan; it won't just happen. Begin with prayer, asking God what you should pursue. List out the disciplines you want to exercise in your life ("I want to pray more regularly" or "I want to have a regular Bible time"). Begin planning times and ways you can implement those disciplines. Be flexible and aware of how your personality will best engage with spiritual disciplines. *Celebration of Discipline* by Richard Foster is a good book to help you get started if you've never practiced spiritual disciplines.

_____

_____

_____

_____

_____

_____

_____

_____

_____

_____

_____

— Chapter 9 —

Owning Your Faith

Learning to Take Risks

*I believe in Christianity as I believe that the sun
has risen: not only because I see it, but because by
it I see everything else.*

C.S. Lewis

*O*h, Lord! Please provide! I really need you to provide!
I found myself desperately uttering this prayer in
my mind before my eyes had even opened. It was
one of those times in life when I couldn't see past tomorrow. I had four grown up children with grown up worries,
a dear and very overworked husband, and a diminishing
bank account. At that moment, my prayer was for the
needs of one of my children's university tuition. Over and
over again I had seen God work, but at that point, after a
year that felt like a boxing match, I found the eyes of my
heart couldn't see around the bend in the road.

I believe all of us come to the moment where we
can't see around the next corner. In fact, in my life, there
have been too many such times to count. It is at those
corners and crossroads that our claim to "have faith" be-

gins to mean something for the real, practical, present world we live in. When I was a young Christian, I think I pictured faith as looking something like the enthusiastic hand-raising worshippers I saw at youth conferences. As I have grown, I have come to see that faith more often looks like the quiet trust and sincere outpouring of a heart before God. It is most visible at moments of crisis, death, hurt, need, and new beginnings. It comes at the moment when we are faced with the choice to trust in ourselves or in the world, to give into despair, or to trust in God to take us beyond what we can imagine and see.

Fear is our natural response to the unknown. That day as I prayed a cold cloud of fear came to me: What if I couldn't send the child to this program she dreamed of for so many years? Had I failed her as a parent? Fear comes to me in the form of a thousand imagined undesirable futures. It comes in the form of what-ifs: What if we start a ministry and it flops? What if the kids resent us for raising them in ministry? What if I am not strong/wise/good enough to do what God has called me to do?

Fear drives us to retreat. In the defensive stance of fear, we try to live in our own strength rather than trusting in the mysterious, beautiful, and powerful work God could do in our lives. But God is well acquainted with our fears. Three-hundred sixty-five times in the Bible, the heartening and seemingly impossible command is uttered, "Do not fear." I learned in the early days of our ministry that if God called me to something, He would never leave me stranded. In Deuteronomy 31:6, God speaks to the Israelites saying, "Be strong and courageous, do not be afraid or tremble at them, for the LORD your God is the one who goes with you. He will not fail you or forsake you." We have the power to be courageous only because we know that wherever we go, God goes with us. Faith is the power.

Another tempting response is to live by formula. As I pondered that morning, I thought of all the systems and methods I should have lived by if I was really a helpful mother. Perhaps I just hadn't done the right thing and it was going to cost my child their education. Trusting in a formula, even if it sounds good, is not living by faith in God, but living by well-intentioned superstition— if I pray, act a certain way, and say the right things, then God will be obligated to respond and grant my desire. That kind of thinking comes too close to the beliefs of idol worshipers in the Old Testament, rather than to followers of the faithful, loving God who revealed Himself in order to be known and worshiped by His people.

God cannot be made to fit into our man-made formulas. In Isaiah, God said, "For My thoughts are not your thoughts, nor are your ways My ways" (55:8). Our God is more gracious and more powerful than any formula we can conjure, and we as image bearers of God are more complex and exciting than any formula can contain. When we reduce faith to a formula we will be disappointed. We will be disappointed in ourselves, thinking if only we had prayed or acted a little differently God would be blessing us. Or, we will be disappointed with God, feeling He has not "lived up to his side of the bargain." God does not negotiate, but we try to.

Finally, perhaps the most tempting option is to live by flesh. Living by your flesh means clenching your teeth and saying, "I can do this. I don't need help." This kind of thinking can be pernicious because we can find ourselves thinking, "I'm persevering for God," when we're actually denying our need for His grace to help us persevere. With this mindset, when we encounter hardships or challenges, rather than admitting our need and asking the Father who cares for us for help, our flesh says to us, "Try harder! Do more! Accomplish it on your own!" God never calls us on a path for which he has not prepared us. This is not to say that living by faith is not hard work; it is! But, as Psalm 127:1 says: "Unless the LORD builds a house, the work of the builders is wasted" (NLT). His very name, Immanuel, means "God with us." When we try to live by flesh, we will burn out as we deny God's life-giving Spirit the opportunity to work.

After praying my prayer that morning, I opened my eyes. I peered out the beautiful bay window by my bed, I rubbed my face across the soft blanket on my bed, and then I laughed. My desperate prayer was prayed as if God had not already provided for me. I suddenly realized that God had already met my needs in a thousand ways. My spiritual amnesia made me want to doubt, but as I rose that morning, it was with a trust that God was providing and would continue to provide whatever my family truly needed.

The day that followed my commitment to trust God was not extraordinary; I cleaned and cooked and laughed with my children. As I look back, I cherish the fact that I have been able to see the hand of God work so powerfully in my lifetime. If I lived only by what was possible in my own power, I would have never taken risks that allowed me to see God's faithfulness. My walk of faith with God has been a mysterious dance of listening, resting, working, and watching as God causes growth. With each crossroad I encounter, I believe even more firmly that God goes before me to prepare the path.

— STUDY THE BIBLE —

Hear the Word
Psalm 105:1-7

1 Oh give thanks to the LORD, call upon His name;
Make known His deeds among the peoples.
2 Sing to Him, sing praises to Him;
Speak of all His wonders.
3 Glory in His holy name;
Let the heart of those who seek the LORD be glad.
4 Seek the LORD and His strength;
Seek His face continually.
5 Remember His wonders which He has done,
His marvels and the judgments uttered by His mouth,
6 O seed of Abraham, His servant,
O sons of Jacob, His chosen ones!
7 He is the LORD our God;
His judgments are in all the earth.

Do the Word

This Psalm was written for a specific purpose—to re-member the work of God on behalf of Israel. It recounts how God made them a people and kept His promises to bring them into the land. As you read the entire psalm in your own Bible, note when the psalmist uses the words "remember" or "remembered." God constantly command-ed the Israelites to recall His faithfulness to them when they forgot, became afraid, and ceased trusting Him. Do you ever forget God's faithfulness in your life? How does it affect your trust in Him? How can you be sure to re-member all that God has done for you? How can you re-call and recount the many promises of God that will re-mind you of God's faithfulness, sovereignty, and power?

Own the Word

Hear the Word
Hebrews 11:1-6

¹ Now faith is the assurance of things hoped for, the conviction of things not seen. ² For by it the men of old gained approval. ³ By faith we understand that the worlds were prepared by the word of God, so that what is seen was not made out of things which are visible. ⁴ By faith Abel offered to God a better sacrifice than Cain, through which he obtained the testimony that he was righteous, God testifying about his gifts, and through faith, though he is dead, he still speaks. ⁵ By faith Enoch was taken up so that he would not see death; AND HE WAS NOT FOUND BECAUSE GOD TOOK HIM UP; for he obtained the witness that before his being taken up he was pleasing to God. ⁶ And without faith it is impossible to please Him, for he who comes to God must believe that He is and that He is a rewarder of those who seek Him.

Do the Word

Read all of Hebrews 11 in your own Bible. It is a grand panoramic picture of faith told through the lives of a faithful "cloud of witnesses" (12:1). It is a series of vignettes of the many different ways we can express faith, but also of the high calling of faith for those who follow God. Read and think about the faithful in this passage, and their faith. What do they all have in common? What do you have in common with them? With which character of faith do you most identify? Does your faith please God (11:6)?

Own the Word

_____

_____

_____

_____

_____

_____

— MAKE A PLAN —

Take three sheets of paper. On the first page, write all of the struggles, worries, hurts, and desires of your heart. Be honest with yourself. On the second page, write down the ways you see God already being faithful in your life. Like the Israelites, take time to remember the ways God has been faithful to you in the past. As you see God's hand in your past, commit your future to Him, believing the words of David: "I was young and now I am old, yet I have never seen the righteous forsaken or their children begging bread" (Psalm 37:25, NIV). On the third page, write out what you think God is calling you to do in faith. Express the ways you want to seek Him and please Him by faith to receive His reward (11:6).

_____

_____

_____

_____

_____

_____

_____

_____

_____

_____

— Chapter 10 —

Owning Your Emotional Health

Tending Your Heart and Investing in Your Soul

Never lose an opportunity of seeing anything beautiful, for beauty is God's handwriting.

RALPH WALDO EMERSON

She called it her treasure chest. I had taken my fifteen year-old son Nathan with me on a special trip to Austria and Poland, the places where I had spent time as a missionary in my twenties. In an open air market in Krakow, I found a special souvenir to take back for Joy. It was a hand-carved box, made of glistening cherry wood, with soft red felt lining on the inside, and a cheerful-looking bear carved onto the top. It was treasure chest for small treasures.

To my delight, Joy loved the box. She carried it with her everywhere collecting in it little treasures she would find. After playing outside, she would come in and place a beautiful bird feather or a shell in the box. After church, she carefully tucked away a bookmark with a prayer on it. After a trip to the Denver Art Museum, she tenderly folded the small print I bought her of a favorite painting and placed it inside. She filled her little box to the brim, and at nights her eyes would shine with delight as she would take out each item to cherish them all. "My treasure box reminds me of all the beauty God has put in the world, Mama!"

Joy's treasure box gave me an image of what it means to cultivate my soul and fill it with truth and beauty. Wherever Joy went, she carried with her a reminder of the light, beauty, and truth of God's goodness. As Christians with the light of Christ in us, we should have hearts full of God's treasures—beauty, grace, and truth—to sustain us in the darkness and to offer to others. To have a rich treasure chest in our hearts, though, we must be intentional about pursuing activities and practices that fill the heart instead of draining it.

God has filled the world with delights for us to encounter, and yet our culture often thinks of beauty, delight, art, and music as secondary pursuits which are perhaps a bit frivolous in comparison to the "real" work of being serious and holy. I would suggest, however, that God wants us to worship him every bit as much in our delight as in our duty.

When we dwell on the extravagant delights God has given us in the world, our hearts are drawn toward Him in worship. When we gaze on God's gifts of beauty to us, we find our eyes drawn away from the ugliness and sin of the world. Perhaps this is why Paul so sincerely exhorts the Philippians saying, "Finally, brethren, whatever is true, whatever is honorable, whatever is right, whatever is pure, whatever is lovely, whatever is of good repute, if there is any excellence and if anything worthy of praise, dwell on these things" (Philippians 4:8). When we fill our hearts with excellence and virtue, we find ourselves with a wealth of God's goodness to offer others from the treasures we have collected.

Just as Joy carefully filled her box, so we must learn to intentionally pursue activities that will fill the treasure chest of our hearts with good things. We should look for ways to fill our hearts, minds, and spirits with goodness, truth, and beauty—the things that inspire us, cause us to worship God, and bring light to others.

I love a good story. Stories are one the of best ways to fill our hearts with beauty. I read hundreds of books to my children when they were young, and I marveled as they were shaped by stories. When we read of the brave heroes in Tolkein's *The Lord of the Rings*, my boys backs stood a little straighter; they wanted to fight evil like Aragorn! As we read of the power of love in *Silas Marner,* I saw them soften and gain a desire to be kind. The stories we put in our hearts—bravery, love, wisdom, goodness—create a storehouse from which the imagination can draw for living a truly "storied" life.

In the first of the two great commandments of Jesus (Matthew 22:36-40), He tells us to love God not just with heart and soul, but also with our minds. Mark Twain famously said, "I never let schooling interfere with my education." Education should not end with whichever diploma you deem to be your last. When we learn about the world and sharpen our minds, our eyes become open to the wisdom with which God created the world. Sharpening our minds can become an act of worship to God. When wisdom and knowledge is stored up in the treasure box of our heart, we are able to draw from it to help give a defense for our faith, marvel at God's creation, and have a well-tempered view of the world around us.

In the same way, when beauty is stored in the heart—music, art, literature, creation—it draws our hearts to worship God, and lifts our spirits from the cynicism and ugliness of modern life. When you listen to a beautiful piece of music, or gaze on a masterpiece of art, or walk in the fresh loveliness of nature, your heart is drawn out of its small occupations to the glory of God. As you offer the beauty stored in your heart, you can draw others into the call of God as well.

— STUDY THE BIBLE —

Hear the Word
Luke 6:45

The good man out of the good treasure of his heart brings forth what is good; and the evil man out of the evil treasure brings forth what is evil; for his mouth speaks from that which fill his heart.

Do the Word

Jesus says that whatever is stored up in our hearts is what will define what comes out of our mouths when we speak to others. To paraphrase the maxim, "We are what we treasure." Take some time to consider what is stored up in your heart. What "good treasure" is already in your heart"? What "good treasure" are you seeking to fill your heart? Is there any "evil treasure" there that "brings forth" negative words that needs to be removed? As you think about the kinds of words you give to others, is there some "good treasure" that you feel you especially need to add to your heart? How can you do that?

Own the Word

_____

_____

_____

_____

_____

_____

ॐ

Hear the Word
Philippians 4:8

Finally, brethren, whatever is true, whatever is honorable, whatever is right, whatever is pure, whatever is lovely, whatever is of good repute, if there is any excellence and if anything worthy of praise, dwell on these things.

Do the Word

The Philippian church had its share of difficulties, but Paul's most fervent instruction to them is to "dwell on"— ponder, think about, reflect on—the good, true, and beautiful. His prescription for their problems was to think about the goodness of God in all its facets. Why do you think Paul places such an emphasis on this? Do you place a similarly strong emphasis on dwelling on good things in your life? When you're faced with challenges or trials, what can you "dwell on" to help give you spiritual perspective? What Bible verses help you do this?

Own the Word

_____

_____

_____

_____

_____

_____

❧

— MAKE A PLAN —

Filling your heart with goodness, truth, and beauty takes intentional effort and time. But according to Jesus and Paul, the benefits will be well worth the investment. Plan into your calendar some specific ways to cultivate your heart, mind, and soul (Matthew 22:37). For your heart, look for something that will fill you with courage and inspire you, perhaps reading an inspiring novel or making a commitment to meet with a life-giving friend once a week or monthly. For your soul, consider ways to delight in beauty, such as a concert, an art gallery, or a walk in a beautiful setting. For your mind, find a book on a subject that interests you, or start a discussion group with friends, or take your children to a natural history museum. Create your own treasure chest to fill with physical reminders of the good, true, and beautiful in your life that you can remember and "dwell on."

_____

_____

_____

_____

_____

_____

_____

_____

_____

_____

_____

_____

— Chapter 11 —

Owning Your Response to Others

Choosing to Overcome: Moving Beyond Hurt

I hold it true, whate'er befall;
I feel it, when I sorrow most;
'Tis better to have loved and lost
Than never to have loved at all.

ALFRED LORD TENNYSON

Facebook confirms Tennyson's poetic lament. I have observed his familiar maxim displayed in modern terms on many walls and news feeds, unsubtly proclaiming the end of another ill-fated teenage relationship, or even a marriage. Sometimes it is said with care, but often it is said carelessly. Sadly, it is too often said as a transition from one coffee-cup conversation to the next with a flip of the hair and a meaningless sigh. You loved. You lost. That's life. You move on. Another love awaits.

Friendship and love is, of course, much more complicated than such simple maxims. In my life, I have loved deeply, and yet I have also had love kick me in the teeth. It is always surprising and it always hurts, especially if it comes from Christians who you expect to be loving and kind.

There have been times where it seemed to me that there was too much losing in the loving. For much of my life I spent years loving imperfectly but with great sincerity, praying and apologizing, and being strong and trying to forgive. Eventually I found myself years down the road with nothing to show but many bruises on my heart. Perhaps you have experienced the same thing. Perhaps for you it was a friend, a sibling, a parent, a partner, or a leader, leaving you wondering if it really is better to have loved and lost.

When experiencing pain engendered by love, whether that be grief from death, betrayal, or rejection, the desire to hide is appealing. Instinctively we hear, "Fooled me once, shame on you; fooled me twice, shame on me." We feel desperately that we need to build fortified walls to protect us from being hurt again in such a way. We recalculate, condemning ourselves for being vulnerable enough to be hurt. We cross our hearts and swear to never be so unwise. We say that we will put up "boundaries" to protect our hearts from unhealthy love, but quickly those boundaries become walls of stone with gates of steel. And we do it all because, in our hearts, deep down, we feel that our love was wasted.

C.S. Lewis, a man deeply familiar with love and loss, wrote of this frustration: "To love at all is to be vulnerable." (*The Four Loves*). As I've pondered the beautiful and truly terrifying reality of the vulnerability in love, I have come to realize that even God is not immune to the pain of love and loss. The story of God's relationship to the world is one of unrequited love. When we learn to be vulnerable and to forgive we get to experience a part of his character. We can learn to love well and release hurt because God first loved and forgave us.

John, the "apostle of love," said: "In this is love, not that we loved God, but that He loved us ..." (1 John 4:10). Love is in the divine DNA of God: "The one who does not love does not know God, for *God is love*" (4:8). The essence of God's nature is love. God loves extravagantly, but never wastefully. God's love is never wasted because it is an expression of his perfect character. When we love, we participate with God and reflect his love. John goes on to say: "No one has ever seen God at any time; if we love one another, God abides in us, and His love is perfected in us" (1 John 4:12).

The apostle Paul famously declared in his tribute to love in 1 Corinthians 13 that love is the greatest virtue. The *agape* love that is the unconditional love of God "never fails" and will never cease. Faith and hope are two of the three greatest virtues he names, but they will no longer be needed when we die. Only love, "the greatest of these" will go with us into eternity. Because that is where the etneral God, who is love, will be.

Love is never wasted. The act of loving proclaims the truest thing in the universe: that God is love. Our love may be weak, foolish, naive, unwise, or even unhealthy, but it is never wasted. Love is the truth that pulses at the heart of reality. It is the lifeblood of every good thing. It does not matter if love is requited, rejected, or abandoned; the true meaning of love stems from the God who is love. When we love we affirm and sing into eternity the marvelous and unfathomable truth that God is love, and we are loved.

Sometimes we lose sight of that truth as we struggle with grief, guilt, and pain. Even in small, feeble attempts at love, God can multiply our offering and bring more than we could ever accomplish ourselves. Even when it seems our love is deflected by an impenetrable heart, God graciously redeems our love from the void. Love leaves a mark, and sometimes it leaves a scar. The greatest love of all bears scars. In Jesus' resurrected body, he bears the scars of his extravagant love. In those scars I find a forgiveness that fills the cracks of my broken attempts at love, and I find solace in a God who knows what it is for His love to be spurned.

When we learn to own our love and our forgiveness, it draws us closer to the heart of God. It is never easy, but it is always worth it. As Paul says, "[Love] rejoices with the truth; bears all things, believes all things, hopes all things, endures all things. Love never fails" (1 Corinthians 13:6b-8a).

— STUDY THE BIBLE —

Hear the Word
Matthew 5:43-48

43 *"You have heard that it was said, 'YOU SHALL LOVE YOUR NEIGHBOR and hate your enemy.' 44 But I say to you, love your enemies and pray for those who persecute you, 45 so that you may be sons of your Father who is in heaven; for He causes His sun to rise on the evil and the good, and sends rain on the righteous and the unrighteous. 46 For if you love those who love you, what reward do you have? Do not even the tax collectors do the same? 47 If you greet only your brothers, what more are you doing than others? Do not even the Gentiles do the same? 48 Therefore you are to be perfect, as your heavenly Father is perfect.*

Do the Word

Jesus places a great emphasis on forgiveness. In this passage, He says that we should love and forgive others generously because God loves and forgives us generously. Have you ever experienced God's love more because you loved or forgave someone? Is there anyone to whom you are having trouble offering forgiveness? When Jesus says we are to "be perfect" as God the Father is perfect, the word he uses (*teleios*) does not mean to be sinless, but rather to be whole, complete, and mature. Our ability to love others is a barometer of our own wholeness and maturity with God. Are there parts of your life that are broken or fragmented that need to become whole so you can love as God loves?

Own the Word

_____

_____

_____

_____

_____

_____

Hear the Word
Ephesians 4:31-32

31 Let all bitterness and wrath and anger and clamor and slander be put away from you, along with all malice. 32 Be kind to one another, tender-hearted, forgiving each other, just as God in Christ also has forgiven you.

Do the Word

Anger and bitterness are deadly poisons. Compare and contrast the positive and negative words Paul uses. When you see negative, unloving qualities in your heart, how can you "put [them] away from you"? Kindness is love in action. What are some kind attitudes and actions you can express toward others, whether those close to you or strangers, to practice a loving approach to life? How does meditating on God's forgiveness in Christ help you have a more tender heart toward others?

Own the Word

_____

_____

_____

_____

_____

_____

— Make a Plan —

Learning to live in forgiveness is a continuous journey, not a single moment. God knows and understands the workings of our hearts, and He honors the desire to forgive. Do you have someone you need to forgive? Take some time and honestly lay your hurts before the Lord. Everyday, each time you think about that person, give them to the Lord in your mind. Ask God to give you the grace and assurance of His love for you so powerfully that you can begin to move on in love.

_____

_____

_____

_____

_____

_____

_____

_____

_____

_____

_____

— Chapter 12 —

Owning Your Integrity

Harvesting a Godly Character

*The greatest legacy one can pass on to one's
children and grandchildren is not money or other
material things accumulated in one's life, but
rather a legacy of character and faith.*

BILLY GRAHAM

A man I once knew was known for his idealism and integrity. He was tried and true, a truth-teller and a grace giver. Everyone knew that when given the opportunity to do wrong, he would choose right. To him it seemed that character was a skill one practiced, and to those who watched his life it seemed apparent that it was a skill he was getting pretty good at. One year, however, an individual bent on smearing his character lied about him publicly and convincingly, putting his ideals and integrity into conflict by the false narrative they spun. Everyone who knew him watched and waited. How would he respond?

C.S. Lewis is famous for his essay "Men Without Chests" (from *The Abolition of Man*). In it, he describes a generation of people without virtue or character because of the rise of relativism and loss of objective truth. In the style of the ancients, he describes the head as the place of knowledge, the heart as the place of passion, and the chest as the place of virtue and character. Only when a person has a well-developed character can they properly put to use knowledge and passion. Without the strength of character developed in the chest, knowledge can become cruel and passion destructive. With character, knowledge becomes wisdom and passion becomes love.

It seems that there are many people without chests in our world. With the constant influx of information provided by the internet, and no effective ways to determine the objectivity or truthfulness of that information, people can develop keen opinions, but not be required either to validate those opinions or to act on them. In the same way, it is easy for us to voice emotional and idealistic claims without doing the hard work of validating our opinions objectively and putting them into actual practice in our lives. Opinion becomes a substitute for character. If we are truly to be full-bodied people who act on the biblical ideals that we hold to be objectively true, then we must practice integrity and grow the muscle of character; we must become men and women with chests.

The essence of character is found in the habitual heart choices of an individual over a long period of time. Character is the constant work of a lifetime and the product of a heart engaged in wisdom, choosing the right thing over and over again. It is like practicing a sport. If you've ever taught a child to catch or throw a ball, you know the moment in which it "clicks." Suddenly, the catcher goes from awkward fumbles to being able to catch the ball almost every time; snagging the ball out of the air becomes an automatic response. Character is the product of good choices made over and over again, so that when the curveballs of life come your way, you can automatically respond in wisdom because that is what you have practiced.

What we practice shapes who we become, and the voices we listen to shape what we will practice. If we are to live lives of character, we must invest in wisdom. One of my mentors once gave me a great quote: "God forgives, but wisdom does not." The heart of wisdom is properly understanding the impact and meaning of our personal choices. The book of Proverbs very clearly delineates good and bad decisions, a practice which is not popular in our day. The purpose of Proverbs is not to create strict rules to live by, but to help the reader live a life of wisdom which brings peace. I do not tell my children "don't go over the speed limit" because I like to impose difficult rules upon them, but because if they do go over the speed limit they will more likely have to pay a ticket or get in a wreck. Wisdom creates healthy hedges around our behavior of what we will and won't do.

As you consistently choose wisdom and live with integrity, you begin to tell a story that others will see. The man I described at the beginning of this chapter exhibits this reality beautifully. As his friends, family, and critics watched and waited, they saw with amazement the results of character exhibited in his life. Having practiced truth, integrity, and love for so long, even in his darkest hour he responded with graciousness, refusing to retaliate, and trusted himself to God. His practice of character protected him and was a testament to others of a life lived well. We should aspire to be people whose character is a testament to life lived faithfully for the love of God.

— STUDY THE BIBLE —

Hear the Word
Proverbs 8:1-11

¹ Does not wisdom call,
And understanding lift up her voice?
² On top of the heights beside the way,
Where the paths meet, she takes her stand;
³ Beside the gates, at the opening to the city,
At the entrance of the doors, she cries out:
⁴ "To you, O men, I call,
And my voice is to the sons of men.
⁵ "O naive ones, understand prudence;
And, O fools, understand wisdom.
⁶ "Listen, for I will speak noble things;
And the opening of my lips will reveal right things.
⁷ "For my mouth will utter truth;
And wickedness is an abomination to my lips.
⁸ "All the utterances of my mouth are in righteousness;
There is nothing crooked or perverted in them.
⁹ "They are all straightforward to him who understands,
And right to those who find knowledge.
¹⁰ "Take my instruction and not silver,
And knowledge rather than choicest gold.
¹¹ "For wisdom is better than jewels;
And all desirable things cannot compare with her.

Do the Word

Proverbs chapters 8 and 9 personifies Wisdom as a woman calling out to the naive, the foolish, and the young men. Read both chapters in your own Bible and note all the benefits that Lady Wisdom offers to those who will listen to her and heed her advice. Lady Wisdom is an active, vivacious person seeking to protect and nurture those willing to sit under her care. How are you seeking wisdom in your life? Do you find yourself living by your whims and feelings, or by God's wisdom and truth? How are you seeking wisdom every day? Do you surround yourself with wise people? Are you a wise person calling out to others?

Own the Word

_____

_____

_____

_____

_____

_____

❧

Hear the Word
Psalm 41:10-13:

10 But You, O LORD, be gracious to me and raise me up,
That I may repay them.
11 By this I know that You are pleased with me,
Because my enemy does not shout in triumph over me.
12 As for me, You uphold me in my integrity,
And You set me in Your presence forever.
13 Blessed be the LORD, the God of Israel,
From everlasting to everlasting.
Amen and Amen.

Do the Word

Having integrity means that you are a whole person—
what you are on the inside is reflected in what you do
outside. Your character and your actions are integrated.
God honors decisions made out of a life of integrity. Why
do you think it is so important to live with character and
integrity? List the ways Christians reflect the character
of Christ to the world. List some ways that you reflect the
character of Christ to your family. When we live with integrity, we are reflecting a God who is faithful and who
has divine integrity. How do you make personal integrity
and character a priority in your life?

Own the Word

_____

_____

_____

_____

_____

_____

— MAKE A PLAN —

Your character and integrity is the legacy you will leave
to your children. What do you want the legacy of your life
to be? Perhaps you want to be remembered for generosi-
ty, honesty, integrity, or love. As you write out what you

OWNING YOUR INTEGRITY

want your legacy to be, consider how you are living your life. Do you currently live in a way that will leave a path of goodness and truth that others behind you can follow? Do you feel you're a whole person whose inside and outside lives are integrated? Commit to God the ways in which you want to grow in character. Ask him to show you where you need His help to grow in character to become a more whole person. Tell a trusted friend the ways in which you want to grow and ask them to pray for you.

_____

_____

_____

_____

_____

_____

_____

_____

_____

_____

_____

_____

107

— Chapter 13 —

Owning Your Choice to Love
Pursuing Life's Most Defining Commitment

*Greater love has no one than this, that one lay
down his life for his friends.*
JESUS (JOHN 15:13)

A friend once called them the "awkward years." In
their early teens, all of my children went through a
time of angst, wrestling, and pimples. From my mama
eyes I could see their struggle; they were burgeoning
adults, wanting to flex their muscles and stretch their
wings, souls wanting deeply to be loved and validated. In
those years I often found myself on my knees begging for
wisdom. The answer I received again and again was this:
They need to know they are loved.

Each of us has a deep longing to be loved—to have
our lives validated, to know that we matter and have a
purpose. We all long to know that there is a place we belong. It is a desire in our hearts because God put it
there. Learning to have a mature love that grows and
gives has to be nurtured and trained. Unconditional love

is not common in most families, and it's not surprising why—it takes an incredible amount of work. When anger is allowed to fester, blame is a constant habit, and loneliness and neglect of needs create strife and depression.

So many moms write to me and say, "My kids fight all the time! They are so selfish. They run all over me!" They say this as though this were an unusual occurrence for motherhood. The truth is we all are self-absorbed, petty, and shallow by nature—*sin* nature, that is! Every family will have clashing personalities—between siblings, between children and parents, and often, to our chagrin as wives, between spouses. No family is immune. For families to grow in grace and to learn to become mature requires training, practice, instruction, and most of all, the kindness of God.

Jesus was a great lover of people. I have always appreciated reading through the Gospel of John and seeing how Jesus meets each person exactly at their heart need. He saw every individual and validated them for who they were—Nathanael sitting under the tree, the woman at the well, Nicodemus seeking truth. In each case, Jesus communicated to the individuals that He saw them in their deepest need, that He loved them, and that they could find belonging in Him. Though Jesus did many miracles, it seems that often what was most compelling to people was His piercing insight into who they were, and His generous love in response to that knowledge.

As people who are marked by God's love for us, the greatest legacy we can leave is one which is marked by our love for God and others. For our children, we should seek to build an environment of love, grace, and belonging so every member of our family can confidently say: "I have a history. I am a Clarkson. We love each other, we belong to each other. We will always have stability because we are a part of this circle of love, spiritual strength, and grace." Whatever your family name, your children could say the same. A child who is given unconditional love, and a safe haven in which to discover that love, will have an inner stability in their soul. They will find strength to face any trial that life brings their way.

I see this in my children as adults. They have chosen challenging arenas—Hollywood, Oxford, New York City—in which to bring the light of Christ to the world. These kinds of places can be quite lonely for a young Christian seeking to hold fast to ideals. However, they draw strength from the deep bonds of love we built into their lives. That deeply ingrained identity—that they belong to our family and to God—stabilizes them in difficult moments. It is the love of Jesus made real and personal.

That identity takes work. Personality differences, age variations, bickering, selfishness, and any number of other negative elements have to be trained away, one day at a time. It's a process. Even when all my kids are back home together during holidays, I know there will likely be a couple of family fusses! But the desire for peace is so strong, because we all need each other, that grace covers the contention and love binds our hearts together.

It is not natural to my personality to love. Anger, impatience, and criticism are all instinctual responses for me to irritating people—especially those in my home! It is only the Spirit living through me that allows God's love to prevail. I have learned to say, "Lord, I am so irritated right now, but I want to be loving and patient. Would you please love through me?" I want to be, but know I am not, a perfect model of love as a mama, so I trust Jesus to keep helping me until I see Him.

Becoming a loving person requires time, correction, forgiveness, grace, and serving—all intentional goals. Love does not grow without a plan, either in yourself or your children. A child can be given all the experiences or things the world has to offer, but if their soul is starving for real love, or filled with the anger of rejection, they will look for love and validation in other, often wrong, places. If your love and God's love fill up their heart, they will not need to look elsewhere.

A mother's love and legacy is one of the most powerful influences in the world in the heart of child. It is an incredible role to fill, and requires choices to serve, give, train, instruct, provide, and encourage. It is a very daily challenge, but it will have eternal consequences. What your children receive from you, they will likely speak into their own lives, and into the lives of others around them. They will love because you loved.

One night Nathan came home from a time with friends. As I observed him in the full force of puberty, I could see that what he needed most was love. I met him with chocolate chip cookies at the door, and invited him to come and talk with me for a minute. He came and sat with me, and through mouthfuls of cookies began to share about his life—hopes and fears, struggles, friendships he cared about, girls he was interested in. As I watched him, I saw my relationship to God—I need so much to know I'm loved before I can be obedient. Years down the road, my relationship with my children is sweet because of the love I invested in their lives. No matter what else you do, let love—unconditional, generous, gracious love—be the most profound commitment you pursue. You love will give your children the gift of truly seeing God's heart for them and the world.

— STUDY THE BIBLE —

Hear the Word
Romans 12:9-21

9 Let love be without hypocrisy. Abhor what is evil; cling to what is good. 10 Be devoted to one another in brotherly love; give preference to one another in honor; 11 not lagging behind in diligence, fervent in spirit, serving the Lord; 12 rejoicing in hope, persevering in tribulation, devoted to prayer, 13 contributing to the needs of the saints, practicing hospitality. 14 Bless those who persecute you; bless and do not curse. 15 Rejoice with those who rejoice, and weep with those who weep. 16 Be of the same mind toward one another; do not be haughty in mind, but associate with the lowly. Do not be wise in your own estimation. 17 Never pay back evil for evil to anyone. Respect what is right in the sight of all men. 18 If possible, so far as it depends on you, be at peace with all men. 19 Never take your own revenge, beloved, but leave room for the wrath of God, for it is written, "VENGEANCE IS MINE, I WILL REPAY," says the Lord. 20 "BUT IF YOUR ENEMY IS HUNGRY, FEED HIM, AND IF HE IS THIRSTY, GIVE HIM A DRINK; FOR IN SO DOING YOU WILL HEAP BURNING COALS ON HIS HEAD." 21 Do not be overcome by evil, but overcome evil with good.

Do the Word

Paul passionately exhorts the church in Rome to create a community shaped by love. How can you cultivate an environment of love in your family? Do you rejoice with those who rejoice and weep with those who weep? This sort of clean and pure love can only come from a heart which knows how deeply and intimately it is cherished by God. Spend some time dwelling on God's love for you.

Own the Word

_____

_____

_____

_____

_____

_____

❦

Hear the Word
1 Corinthians 13

1 If I speak with the tongues of men and of angels, but do not have love, I have become a noisy gong or a clanging cymbal. 2 If I have the gift of prophecy, and know all mysteries and all knowledge; and if I have all faith, so as to remove mountains, but do not have love, I am nothing. 3 And if I give all my possessions to feed the poor, and if I surrender my body to be burned, but do not have love, it profits me nothing.

4 Love is patient, love is kind and is not jealous; love does not brag and is not arrogant, 5 does not act unbecomingly; it does not seek its own, is not provoked, does not take into account a wrong suffered, 6 does not rejoice in unrighteousness, but rejoices with the truth; 7 bears all things, believes all things, hopes all things, endures all things.

8 Love never fails; but if there are gifts of prophecy, they will be done away; if there are tongues, they will cease; if there is knowledge, it will be done away. 9 For we know in part and we prophesy in part; [10] *but when the perfect comes, the partial will be done away.* [11] *When I was a child, I used to speak like a child, think like a child, reason like a child; when I became a man, I did away with childish things.* [12] *For now we see in a mirror dimly, but then face to face; now I know in part, but then I will know fully just as I also have been fully known.* [13] *But now faith, hope, love, abide these three; but the greatest of these is love.*

Do the Word

This beautiful tribute to love, often used to mark wedding ceremonies, bears repeating in any setting. Read this passage with new eyes. Imagine what someone who loved you this way would look like. How would you respond to their love? How do you know that God loves you this way? How does His love for you influence your love for others? How does thinking about Paul's descriptions of what love looks like in this passage help you change your response toward those around you? What makes love, as Paul says, the "greatest" of the virtues?

Own the Word

_____

_____

_____

_____

_____

_____

— MAKE A PLAN —

Love is an action, not just a feeling. Make a "love does" plan to express love to someone this week—a family member, a friend, someone at church, even a stranger. Pray about who in your life God could be asking you to love for His sake. Write out specific things you will do, or words or thoughts that you will say, to truly show each person on your "love does" list that they are loved.

_____

_____

_____

_____

_____

_____

_____

_____

_____

_____

_____

— Chapter 14 —

Owning the Atmosphere of Your Home

Cultivating a Sense of Place

*Love begins at home, and it is not how much we
do ... but how much love we put in that action.*

MOTHER TERESA

Our home is a place of comings and goings. For
much of my life I was under the impression that,
eventually, everyone in my life would be settled. So far,
this has never been the case. Yet somehow in the midst
of the comings and goings, our home remains a place of
rest, beauty, and soul refreshment. It's not just a house,
but a home.

One summer when Joy had returned from a very
depleting year at college, Sarah was champing at the bit
to be on her way to England for the fall, Nathan was
hard at work on a movie, and Joel was in transition between two different places. Each heart was filled with a
hundred different preoccupations, but as everyone sat
down at our familiar dining room table, a freshly-made
feast laid out before them, they were drawn back into the

life-giving atmosphere of the Clarkson home. In this place, my children had grown, learned, and been nurtured, and now as they returned from their adventures in the wild world, they had come again as adults to grow, learn, and renew their souls.

One night, with her weary head on my lap, Joy said, "Mama, I'm so thankful for this home. It's a place where I can come, rest, and be prepared to go back out into the world again." Home is written deep in the longings of our hearts, and cultivating home is a work of a lifetime. The grace of a home is its ability to shelter and to nourish, but we live in an increasingly homeless world. I don't mean that people lack houses (though some certainly struggle with this), but that many people lack homes within their houses—they do not have a place to rest, be sheltered, be nourished, and be sent out knowing they are loved.

I believe everyone has an innate longing for home; we yearn for a place that is prepared just for us, a place where we are anticipated. Jesus said to his disciples, "I go to prepare a place for you" (John 14:3), and spoke of a house with many rooms. In the Old Testament, the prophets spoke frequently of the feast God is preparing for the world when all is redeemed. Whenever I read these passages, I am struck by their appeal to the deep longing we all have for a place to belong. If Christ is in us, then the way we cultivate our homes mediates His lovingkindness to others. The task of cultivating a home is not simply housewife endeavors to keep things tidy, but a deeply spiritual act of worship that has the potential to change souls for all of eternity.

Home is the place best-designed to explore and shape what we think about the world. In my life, I loved creating an environment of life for my small children. I scattered our home with beauty, art, music, healthy food, and nature. Though we moved a great deal, I always intentioned to make our home one of life and love, and wherever we went, we carried our ideals of home with us. Our children felt safe and loved, and in that safety they explored and learned.

When we as empowered parents cultivate our homes, we create a space in which our children can try new things, make mistakes, and learn the truth in safety without outside pressures. Not only does such a home nurture its own family, it changes every person who enters its doors. As the Holy Spirit blows through the house, life and love permeate its atmosphere. It is a garden in which the soul of every person who enters it is watered and tended to with care.

As my children grew into adults, I began to see home as a fortress from which strong warriors were sent out. Though I was always sad to see my children go, I delighted in knowing that they would bring light to the world. The grace that they received in our home enabled, protected, and motivated them to bring grace to the environments in which they engaged. The true purpose of my home was to send anyone who entered it out with more grace and strength. A home which never opens its doors and airs its ideals about truth is a home where the air of goodness becomes stale. One of the great dignities of a home is its ability to send out those who have been nurtured within its walls, halls, and rooms.

Just as a home sends people out in strength, it receives people back who have become weary. Over the years my children have often returned to my home in times of sadness, exhaustion, and depletion. In my home, I try to model Jesus who said, "Come to Me, all who are weary and heavy-laden, and I will give you rest" (Matthew 11:28). One of the glories of a home is its role as a safe harbor for weary souls. The world is a difficult place, but in the walls of an intentionally welcoming home, a soul can find the warmth, love, and grace that lies close to the heart of Jesus.

As the end of my summer approached, I sent Joy off on a beautiful morning to a semester in Oxford. With bags packed and traveling outfit on, I made Joy her last cup of tea before leaving. As we sat in the lovely early rays just emerging into daylight, with a hint of a fall breeze finally beginning to blow through the porch, I looked at my girl and smiled. The dark circles and furrowed brows that hung heavy on her young face at the beginning of the summer were gone.

"What a summer, Mama. I'm sad to leave home again, but this summer has healed and refreshed me. I'm ready to be sent out."

— STUDY THE BIBLE —

Hear the Word
Proverbs 14:1

The wise woman builds her house, but the foolish tears it down with her own hands.

Do the Word

Houses are built with labor and materials. A home is built with dedication, love, and time. What do you think it means to be a wise woman who "builds her house"?

What are the ways that a foolish woman "tears it down"? Why do you think that the idea of home is mentioned so frequently in the Bible? How has home influenced your life and your experience of God and the world? What can you do to begin building a home in your house?

Own the Word

_____

_____

_____

_____

_____

_____

❧

Hear the Word
Isaiah 32:16-18

16 _Then justice will dwell in the wilderness_
And righteousness will abide in the fertile field.
17 _And the work of righteousness will be peace,_
And the service of righteousness, quietness
and confidence forever.
18 _Then my people will live in a peaceful habitation,_
And in secure dwellings and in undisturbed resting
places ...

Do the Word

Isaiah says that the sign of God's presence will be a "peaceful habitation," or a home. Why do you think this is a sign of God's presence? Have you ever been in a home that enabled you to tangibly feel the presence and love of God? Describe that home. What specific elements of a home can help to foster peace? How can you bring God's life and peace into your home so that it becomes a "peaceful habitation"?

Own the Word

_____

_____

_____

_____

_____

_____

— MAKE A PLAN —

Cultivating a home can be a work of many years. The home in which I currently live has become a haven, but only over time. Every year, especially during summer, I have made it a goal to beautify our home in some way, big or small. Now, ten years down the road, it is a life-giving place to the entire Clarkson family, and others. Is your home a life-giving environment? Have you cultivated your spaces? Take some time to think about ways you could nurture the atmosphere of goodness, truth, and beauty in your home. Create a plan to accomplish them, even if it will take some time. Don't get overwhelmed by the vastness of the task ahead; just beautify one step at a time. This could mean anything from decorating a special place for having one-on-one tea with your children, to making a commitment to cook more homemade meals, to inviting your lonely neighbor over for a delicious dinner. Consider how you might make your home a place which cultivates, comforts, and sends back out those who enter it.

Chapter 15

Owning Your Marriage

Building a Legacy over a Lifetime

*What, then, is marriage for? It is for helping each
other to become our future glory-selves, the new
creations that God will eventually make us.*

TIMOTHY KELLER (*THE MEANING OF MARRIAGE*)

With intentionality and thoughtfulness in his eyes,
Clay entered the room with an article in hand.
Passionate about all issues, more engaged in world news
than I, a knowing smile crept across my heart.

I thought to myself, *I know this man. He cares deeply about all things that really matter in the world. How
blessed I am to have a man who engages in life and truth,
and who wants to discuss it or write about it.* I knew that
Clay cared deeply about truth.

"Let's sit on the deck. I'll make us a cup of tea and
slice a piece of lemon-blueberry cake!" As the wind gently
blew through the pine trees just out of the reach of our
wicker chairs, Clay read me the essay he had written in
response to a controversial current topic being discussed
among Christians on the Internet.

I was amazed at his ability to clearly articulate the issues, the beauty of words that, like a sword, pierced my heart with truth and conviction, while simultaneously bringing me a renewed admiration for his ability to write about deep issues with such grace.

This introverted, quiet man that God had given to me was *my* man. Over many years of life pressures, I have learned to be attentive to his personality, be aware of what he cares about and what frustrates him, and be invested in his concerns and hopes. In turn, he has learned to do the same for me. But it took me many years to understand his ways and to appreciate his gifts and drives.

As a young wife, wrapped up in my own understanding of the world, I often unintentionally provoked arguments and had squabbles with Clay—like any young couple would. As a passionate, enthusiastic idealist, I eventually realized that I put pressure on him to recreate himself in my image. The concept of partnership, of two diverse lives blending together into one, had not yet taken hold of my understanding.

Years of hammering out the differences between us helped me to recognize that we both brought abundant gifts to the table of our family's life together. When I combined my strengths with his, rather than resenting him for not being more like me, I found that the Holy Spirit began to weave us together into a beautiful, unified tapestry.

After over three decades of marriage, I am able to recognize more fully that if either of us had been the only influence in our children's lives, they would have received an imbalanced training. Together, Clay and I made an amazing, dynamic duo. Unity amidst diversity.

Most marriages start out with at least some idealism and romantic expectation. Mine was no different. Clay won me with bouquets of yellow roses (I was his yellow rose of Texas), romantic cards, and lots of dinners out. And then there was life—seventeen moves, six internationally; four children and three miscarriages; morning sickness all nine months of every pregnancy, and a near-death experience from blood loss during one miscarriage. Yes, life threw everything and the kitchen sink at us. We have had deaths of family members, car wrecks, financial challenges, illnesses, three home floods and a fire, church splits, conflicts with relatives, ministry frustrations, and lots and lots of stress.

Nothing quite prepared me, as a very immature, untrained young woman, to know how to bear all of the stresses we would face just by being a family.

And yet, I had been taught to seek God's Word, to pray, and to obey and live in wisdom. Early on, I learned that my marriage was a place of worship where I could either seek to bring God's love, healing, and grace every day because of my love for Him, or I could just live as a hypocrite and say that I was committed to God and would serve Him—except in marriage, because that was just asking too much!

I think there is a point where every godly women has to say, "This is the reality of the puzzle I have been given in my life and in my marriage. I can either live and bring light, life, beauty, and redemption into my situation, and bring godly love to my relationship with this husband, or I can live in disappointment." The reality is that in a fallen world there will always be stress and sin. Indeed, there are some broken things in our lives that will always hurt this side of heaven.

All children long to see their moms and dads love each other and be partners in life. The reality is that all marriages are filled with potential challenges, difficulties, and disappointments. How a woman responds to those difficulties within her marriage will determine whether or not it will be a place where the light and beauty of God's love will be shown.

"Above all, keep fervent in your love for one another, because love covers a multitude of sins" (1 Peter 1:8). "[Put] on love, which is the perfect bond of unity" (Colossians 3:14)." "By this all men will know you are My disciples, if you have love for one another" (John 13:35). All of these verses apply to marriage as well as to all relationships of life.

As Clay and I have cultivated this kind of grace-giving love, it has bloomed in the hearts of our children. They know we are not perfect, but they believe in a strong love that is the oxygen of commitment and the way we live in our home. All of our children feel that we are a part of a community of love because they have been drawn through all the seasons by getting back to the center—loving actively, using words of life, and sowing the seeds of kindness.

Foundations of strength and longevity start with a commitment in the heart: Am I willing to accept this story, this husband, these children, and cultivate God's story through my life today? When I accept our limitations and lean into our story with grace and love, it can become a love story worth telling to generations to come?.God joins our commitment and sprinkles His grace and goodness on it. Our acceptance of life along with His grace becomes a miracle of His work that will last for generations.

— STUDY THE BIBLE —

Hear the Word
Genesis 2:15-25

¹⁵ Then the Lord God took the man and put him into the garden of Eden to cultivate it and keep it.
¹⁶ The LORD God commanded the man, saying, "From any tree of the garden you may eat freely; ¹⁷ but from the tree of the knowledge of good and evil you shall not eat, for in the day that you eat from it you will surely die."
¹⁸ Then the LORD God said, "It is not good for the man to be alone; I will make him a helper suitable for him." ¹⁹ Out of the ground the LORD God formed every beast of the field and every bird of the sky, and brought them to the man to see what he would call them; and whatever the man called a living creature, that was its name. ²⁰ The man gave names to all the cattle, and to the birds of the sky, and to every beast of the field, but for Adam there was not found a helper suitable for him. ²¹ So the LORD God caused a deep sleep to fall upon the man, and he slept; then He took one of his ribs and closed up the flesh at that place. ²² The LORD God fashioned into a woman the rib which He had taken from the man, and brought her to the man. ²³ The man said, "This is now bone of my bones, And flesh of my flesh; She shall be called Woman, Because she was taken out of Man."
²⁴ For this reason a man shall leave his father and his mother, and be joined to his wife; and they shall become one flesh. ²⁵ And the man and his wife were both naked and were not ashamed.

Do the Word

From the very beginning God created marriage to delight and fulfill humans and to glorify Himself. In reading this passage, what would you say is the ultimate intention of marriage in God's design for man and woman? When God saw Adam he said, "It is not good for the man to be alone." How do you see that you and your husband are better together than alone? How do you partner together in living for God's kingdom? How do you "subdue" and "rule over" (Genesis 1:28) your world together?

Own the Word

_____

_____

_____

_____

_____

_____

Hear the Word
Hosea 2:19-20, 23

19 *"I will betroth you to Me forever;*
Yes, I will betroth you to Me in righteousness and in justice,
In lovingkindness and in compassion,
20 *And I will betroth you to Me in faithfulness.*
Then you will know the LORD.
23 *... And I will say to those who were not My people,*
'You are My people!'
And they will say, 'You are my God!'"

Do the Word

The whole book of Hosea models the relationship of marriage as an image of the love and faithfulness of God. Unlike anything else, the marriage relationship models covenant faithfulness—a willingness to love, forgive, and be faithful no matter what comes. Your marriage is a reflection of that kind of love. How does this view of marriage change the way you approach your commitment to your marriage? What is the story you are telling with your faithfulness and love of your spouse? What can you do to help make your story together one worth telling to future generations?

Own the Word

_____

_____

_____

_____

_____

_____

— MAKE A PLAN —

Write down on a piece of paper the strengths and weaknesses of your marriage. It's always easier to think of weaknesses, so spend extra time to identify the unique strengths in your marriage relationship. Pray through the list, thanking God for the strengths, and asking for His help with the weaknesses. Then, make two (just two) very practical and realistic goals for how you can improve your marriage and contribute to nurturing the faithfulness and love in your relationship. Write out a plan below for how and when you will work on each of those goals.

_____

_____

_____

_____

_____

_____

_____

_____

_____

_____

_____

— Chapter 16 —

Owning Your Motherhood

Shaping Generations to Come

I've learned that my influence on my children is limited only by the smallness of my dreams and my lack of commitment to the Lord and his purposes.

SALLY CLARKSON (*THE MISSION OF MOTHERHOOD*)

Sipping coffee from a mug on a snowy Colorado day brought pleasure to my weary soul. As the mother of two children under three years old, I was in need of a break. Clay volunteered to take Sarah, almost three, and Joel, just shy of six months, for a couple of hours so that I could visit with a friend of mine I had met as a young missionary in Eastern Europe.

She was eight years older than me, and much further along the path of motherhood with her children approaching teen years at the time. I deeply valued her wisdom and had always looked forward to our times together in the past. And yet today, something she said to me did not sit well with my spirit. Always I had longed for encouragement in my role as a mom, but her words made my heart feel uneasy.

"Sally, you are so talented in ministry and such a great speaker. You and Clay should just decide not to have any more children. You have your daughter and now a son, so you don't need any more kids. It would be a waste of your ministry skills and training to further distract yourself with the burden of more children."

Our time ended shortly after her unsolicited and unexpected counsel, but I couldn't shake the dark feeling her words had brought. The next morning, I rose early, before the two little ones called for me, and began to look up scripture about motherhood and children.

"God blessed them; and God said to them, 'Be fruitful and multiply, and fill the earth ...'" (Genesis 1:28).

The first command from God as he blessed Adam and Eve was to have children. If God considered this a part of His blessing then, didn't he mean it for all times? And wasn't it important since God gave it as a part of His mandate to "subdue" the earth? I realized that every family is different, some couples will not be able to have children, and we are all called to live by faith. But how could my public ministry compare to the immeasurable value and blessing of having children and being a family?

"Now the man called his wife's name Eve, because she was the mother of all the living" (Genesis 3: 20).

Eve's nature as the first woman, and as the "mother of all the living," was established before the fall. Motherhood was an important part of God's design for man and woman before sin ever came into the world. God's original intent for motherhood was not changed by the fall. This seemed to elevate motherhood biblically.

As I continued to read through the scriptures, I constantly saw that children and family were of eternal value to God. Jesus was clear about His heart for children: "... do not hinder [the children] from coming to Me; for the kingdom of heaven belongs to such as these" (Matthew 19:14). The Spirit showed me verses that affirmed God's design for mothers, and reflected the very nature of God in the role of motherhood.

Since I had been trained to disciple adults as a missionary, I began to realize that God had created me as a mother to disciple my children, the future adults in my own home. The more I have studied this topic in thirty-plus years of motherhood, the more I have become convinced of the importance of a mother as a disciple maker. That has inspired me to write six books on motherhood, and I am not sure I am finished yet! I have come to believe that mothers have the power to civilize nations by taking seriously the opportunity they have to disciple their children and to raise them to be godly leaders.

Though my friend had good intentions in giving her advice, I instinctively knew that childbearing was imbued with eternal significance—raising children, building a home, and passing on a legacy of righteousness was part of God's eternal design for the family. My investment in my children as a strategic ministry of faith was no less important than the ministry I had outside of my home. That encounter, and the study that followed, paved the way for us to decide to have more children, and for me to put aside the demands of public ministry in order to focus on the new personal ministry in my home.

Now, as a mother who has raised four children from birth into adulthood, I can affirm that engaging my life and faith in the lives of my children has been the most fulfilling and fruitful work I have ever pursued. I have never regretted the decision to do less ministry, have more children, and give myself fully to the ministry of raising them. It was a challenge every day, but giving up my life to serve my precious children formed my character and faith as God's child.

My investment in my children was about more than all the routine work of motherhood, and even more than my spiritual influence as a discipler. In the bigger picture of my life at home, I was civilizing my children, and shaping their hearts and lives. I was cooperating with God to mold them into well-rounded adults.

To "civilize" means "to create a high level of culture" and "to teach somebody to behave in a more socially, morally and culturally acceptable way" (Merriam-Webster Dictionary). I believe home, by God's design, is the fountain of civilization, and the incubator of mental, moral, and spiritual character, appetites, habits, and values.

"Mothers, you are the divinely-appointed teachers and guides of your children; and any attempt to free yourselves of this duty is in direct opposition to the will of God. If you neglect them, the consequences are swift and sure. ... Spend most of your time with your children. Sleep near them, attend and dress and wash them; let them eat with their mother and father; be their companion and friend in all things and at all times."

The above quotation was gleaned from a wonderful book a friend gave to me called *Golden Thoughts on Mother, Home, and Heaven*, published in 1878. The words still resonate, especially in today's culture where the imagination for how mothers can affect the overall well-being of the soul of the next generation has been lost.

In the absence of a clear, biblical vision for their children and homes, mothers will often replace conviction, vision, and engagement with activities and distractions for their children. They will rush around to an endless list of lessons and experiences, or buy the currently popular curriculum, or get the latest technological devices. But that kind of life is ultimately unfulfilling. However, when a home is rich with excellence and real life—great classic literature, passionate Bible devotions, rousing dinner-table discussions, sumptuous and tasty meals, lots of love and affection—the children in it will be shaped by those things. Their moral and spiritual compass will be set by the power of a magnetic home life.

God created the home and family as a place to nurture genius, excellence, graciousness, and civility. However, there is no turnkey program to purchase that will make that happen. It happens when the soul of a mother, through the power of the Holy Spirit, chooses to personally mentor, disciple, and influence her children. It happens when her spirit is fully engaged at the deepest levels with her children's spirits, and her heart is fully committed to enriching her home with goodness, truth, and beauty.

When the invisible strings of a mother's heart are tied to the hearts of her children through loving sacrifice and nurture, the foundations of a nation will become more secure and stable. When she is living well in her God-ordained role, her impact is irreplaceable and necessary to the spiritual formation of children who will be the future adults of the next generation.

Motherhood is a noble quest and a strategic mission. Mothers are God's guards for children's hearts in a fallen world; His hands for giving love to children; His words for speaking comfort and wisdom; His voice for showing the way; His embrace for affirming value and acceptance. May you cling to His love for you, as you are the conduit of His love and grace to your children.

— STUDY THE BIBLE —

Hear the Word
Psalm 127:3-5

3 Behold, children are a gift of the LORD,
The fruit of the womb is a reward.
4 Like arrows in the hand of a warrior,
So are the children of one's youth.
5 How blessed is the man whose quiver is full of them;
They will not be ashamed
When they speak with their enemies in the gate.

Do the Word

Several times in the Psalms, children are described as a gift from the Lord. How do you see your children as a "gift" from the Lord? In what way is your child a "reward" to you? How does seeing children as a gift and a reward rather than as a burden or an obligation change the way you approach your parenting? How do you experience God's "blessing" as a parent?

Own the Word

_____

_____

_____

_____

_____

Hear the Word
Genesis 12:1-3

1 Now the LORD said to Abram, "Go forth from your country, and from your relatives and from your father's house, to the land which I will show you; 2 and I will make you a great nation, and I will bless you, and make your name great; and so you shall be a blessing; 3 and I will bless those who bless you, and the one who curses you I will curse. and in you all the families of the earth will be blessed."

Do the Word

God promises to Abram that all the nations will be blessed through him. This was eventually fulfilled through Jesus, but also through his immediate family. Why do you think God chose an earthly family to be the conduit of His grace to all people? What do you think it meant to Abram that his family would be an extension of God's blessings to all people? How does that shape the way you think about the legacy of your own parenting?

Own the Word

_____

_____

_____

_____

_____

_____

— MAKE A PLAN —

Your home is a kingdom in which you get to faithfully rule and invest in the family God has given you. Make a time to talk with your spouse about what sort of legacy, family culture, and spiritual heritage you want your family to be known for and defined by. Make a list of the highest priorities to your family. First, pick one priority that you think will help "civilize" your children and plan how to implement it in your family life (such as music, meal time habits, and such). Then, think of a Christian tradition for one of your priorities that will influence your children spiritually and plan how to institute it weekly, monthly, or annually (such as an annual family day).

_____

_____

_____

_____

_____

_____

_____

_____

_____

_____

_____

— Chapter 17 —

Owning the Influence Your Life Can Make

Living Intentionally to Leave a Legacy of Faith

There is no single way to serve God, but the point is this: We each have only one life to live to tell a story about Him, about His ways, about His love. And if we are Christ followers, then God calls us to use our gifts, to exercise our faith, and to become salt and light right where we are.

SALLY CLARKSON (*OWN YOUR LIFE*)

Not long ago I went for a stroll around my yard. As I slowly walked around the garden, I watered the plants and flowers, trimmed my bushes, and enjoyed the cool at the end of a hot summer day. I ended my leisurely time by standing on the hill behind our house. From where I stood, I could see our home, the path leading into the woods, and the foothills of the Rockies lit up with the tender hues of the sunset. But my eyes were caught by something at my feet—a sea of flush pink flowers. On this spot four years before I had helped Joy grow her own small garden. We had planted and nourished it then, but to my knowledge the spot had lain barren for three years while Joy was away at college. Yet, here it was, the fruit of our labor four years hence. I cut a generous bunch of the flowers and placed the bouquet on our table.

Gardens have always reminded me of the profound realities of life and death. Each year I watch as spring brings forth its irrepressible loveliness, reminding me of the beauty and youth of my daughters. Summer brings lovely greens and juicy fruits, and mosquitos, reminding me of my buzzing busy years with young children in tow. And then there is fall, with its dulcet tones and a certain loveliness in its gradual dying.

It all makes me think of 1 Peter 1:24: "All flesh is like the grass, and all its glory like the flower of grass. The grass withers, and the flower falls off, but the word of the Lord endures forever." I am still strong, but I feel in myself the reality of autumn—like the leaves of fall, I too am in the process of gradually dying. It makes me contemplate what I will leave behind? What will be the fruit of my life? What is the story my children and my children's children will tell?

I think our culture is terrified of death. We shield our eyes from all that is not young and healthy, we hide our parents away in nursing homes. But didn't Jesus say, "[U]nless a grain of wheat falls into the earth and dies, it remains alone; but if it dies, it bears much fruit?" (John 12:24). As I enter the autumn of my life, I want to do so with an eye for legacy and eternity. Someday, I will be gone, but what story will I leave behind? Will I leave a legacy of faith, truth, and love?

One of my children's dear friends works at a Christian camp every summer. It was started by his grandfather not long after the World War II. Watching the tides of culture pull many into a compromise of values, this man had in his heart the desire to pass on a love of Jesus and a value for the preciousness of His words. Each summer, he took his children and their friends up for a week in the mountains. In between mirth-filled marsh-mallow roasting, gaspingly beautiful hikes, and the comfort of familial friendship, he would call his children to a life of faith, challenge them to be deep disciples, and impress upon them the endless love that God had for them. Over time some of the children who originally attended the camp grew into adulthood and taught their own children, and so on into further generations.

Though our friend's grandfather passed away, the camps became a living legacy of his passion for the Lord, and his desire to spiritually encourage the next generation. He left a legacy of discipleship, a story of generous love for the people he mentored, and the fruit of many years of investment in people's hearts. Because of his simple vision, and his plan and determination to make it happen, literally hundreds of youth have given their lives to Christ through his summer camps.

If I could leave you with one thought to take away from this book, it would be this: What is the legacy you will leave? It is easy to become consumed in the never-ending demands of our day-to-day worlds. Life can feel like a batting cage where the ball machine is broken, leaving us frantically swinging at nonstop wayward pitches. The only way to change that is to make some new, and sometimes hard, decisions.

My challenge to you in this book is to own your life. Not just so you can be happy or feel more self-actualized, but so, when you reach the end of it, you will leave behind a life rich with the grace of God—a family marked by the deep love you gave to them from the riches of God's love in your life, and a story of faithfulness that gives everyone after you a picture of what it means to live "in a manner worthy of the gospel" (Philippians 1:27).

— STUDY THE BIBLE —

Hear the Word
Matthew 631-34

[31] *Do not worry then, saying, 'What will we eat?' or 'What will we drink?' or 'What will we wear for clothing?'* [32] *For the Gentiles eagerly seek all these things; for your heavenly Father knows that you need all these things.* [33] *But seek first His kingdom and His righteousness, and all these things will be added to you.* [34] *"So do not worry about tomorrow; for tomorrow will care for itself. Each day has enough trouble of its own.*

Do the Word

Jesus taught priorities in the Sermon on the Mount. Our first priority is to seek His kingdom and His righteousness. How are you seeking God's kingdom? How are you seeking His truth and wisdom? What priorities do you need to change to own your life for His glory? What worries do you need to stop worrying about?

Own the Word

_____

_____

_____

_____

_____

_____

Hear the Word
2 Timothy 4:7-8

⁷ I have fought the good fight, I have finished the course, I have kept the faith; ⁸ in the future there is laid up for me the crown of righteousness, which the Lord, the righteous Judge, will award to me on that day; and not only to me, but also to all who have loved His appearing.

Do the Word

Near the end of his life, Paul was confident that he had lived a life worthy of God's honor. When you are older, can you imagine being able to agree with Paul's assessment for your own life, that you "fought the good fight" and "kept the faith"? What would prevent you from saying that of yourself? As you ponder all that you have read and considered in this study guide, what are the dreams, desires, and legacies that God has put on your heart to begin building in your life, marriage, and family?

Own the Word

_____

_____

_____

_____

_____

_____

— MAKE A PLAN —

Spend a few minutes in prayer. Commit your entire journey, past and present, to the Lord—your hopes and fears, the guilt that nags at you, and the pride that steals grace out of your life. Entrust God with your desires, and acknowledge your need for Him. Thank Him for His grace for you and His faithfulness in all elements of your life. When you finish praying, write down truths and blessings that you are grateful to God for. And then go with the knowledge that God walks with you into the continuation of an exciting journey, to sanctify you and make you into a woman after His own heart.

_____

_____

_____

_____

_____

_____

_____

_____

_____

_____

_____

_____

— Afterword —

Owning Your Life

Because Your Life Matters

*So what about you? What kind of legacy do you
want to leave? What life messages are worth
living and dying for? You have a God-sized story
to tell, a destiny to live into! Yet you must choose
to take a step of faith toward Him. Now is the
time; today is the day. Own your life.*

SALLY CLARKSON (*OWN YOUR LIFE*)

I wrote this book because I firmly believe that your life
matters. It matters to God, to your husband, to your
children, to your extended family, to those you influence
and touch. And it matters to me. Your life matters because of a common reality we share. We share in the life
of Christ together, and He makes our lives matter,

Jesus poured His life into twelve flesh and blood
men two thousand years ago, and those relationships
have become a pattern to me and to all who follow Christ
for how to live a life that matters. For three short years,
Jesus loved the select group of men He called His disciples, taught them the things of God, shared everything
with them, and walked with them as friends. And those
men—His friends—would turn the world upside down
with His life-giving messages.

Mentoring students on college campuses helped me grow in experience and wisdom on my journey of personal ministry to women. My journey of development accelerated with seven years of ministry in Austria and Communist Eastern Europe, encouraging women of all ages to live for Christ and His kingdom.

Then came marriage and children—a new mission field. Home became a vibrant laboratory for growing the life of Christ in our family. Jesus has been the spiritual oxygen we've breathed for over three decades. How I loved watching lights come on in the minds of my children as they understood truths about God, His kingdom, and His purposes. As they grew strong in faith and embraced dreams of how to invest their lives and talents for God, I was filled with a deep sense of fulfillment. But I was also filled with a growing sense of responsibility.

I wanted to pass on what I had learned about motherhood and discipleship to other moms. That desire birthed a unique speaking and conference ministry. For over twenty years I have had the privilege of speaking the Word and heart of God to women in our annual Mom Heart Conferences. Women come from all over the country and from all around the world because they are hungry for truth and spiritual encouragement. They want to know that what they are doing matters—that all that they have given up to have children, all they are sacrificing to build a home, and all they are investing their lives in will matter. Like all of us, they want to know that they matter to God, and that they matter to this world.

When I consider all the women I'm able to encourage in my personal ministry, at each of those special conferences, and through my books, I know these are all lives that matter deeply to God. When I was a young woman just starting my journey of faith, I never envisioned having such a widespread ministry to countless thousands of women, but I have been faithful to own the ministry that God entrusted to me. And I take very seriously the privilege I have to speak faith, hope, love, grace, and truth into the hearts of so many wonderful women. I feel the same weight of responsibility in the writing ministry God has given to me.

So as I close this *Own Your Life Bible Study Guide and Planner* with the final encouragement that "your life matters," I want you to know that that truth comes out of many years of real ministry. It is not just a convenient line to write into a book; it is a deep and personal conviction to speak into your heart. If we were able to meet over a hot cup of tea in the candle-lit quiet of my living room, it is what I would want to make sure you knew before you left my home. If you know that your life matters, then I know God is there working in your own life and through your unique story.

Since we probably won't be able to share that tea, I'd like to imagine where you might be as you read these final words. I would grasp your hands, look in your eyes, and give you these words personally and sincerely as my benediction for you:

> *I believe that the seeds of faith you plant will bless generations to come. I believe the story you tell will write the truth of God's love on the hearts of your spouse, children, and community. I believe that the quiet, faithful decisions you make are seen and honored by God. I believe the world will be marked by the kingdom of God because of your life.*

I hope one day to be standing next to you in heaven, and to hear our Savior and King say to each of us: "Well done, good and faithful servant! You have been faithful with a few things; I will put you in charge of many things. Come and share your master's happiness!" (Matthew 25:23). Let us walk together into the light of God's love for us, and let us live lives worthy of His calling that will make a difference. That will matter.

Let me leave you with Paul's beautiful prayer recorded in Ephesians 3:14-21. It is my prayer for you.

[14] For this reason I bow my knees before the Father, [15] from whom every family in heaven and on earth derives its name, [16] that He would grant you, according to the riches of His glory, to be strengthened with power through His Spirit in the inner man, [17] so that Christ may dwell in your hearts through faith; and that you, being rooted and grounded in love, [18] may be able to comprehend with all the saints what is the breadth and length and height and depth, [19] and to know the love of Christ which surpasses knowledge, that you may be filled up to all the fullness of God. [20] Now to Him who is able to do far more abundantly beyond all that we ask or think, according to the power that works within us, [21] to Him be the glory in the church and in Christ Jesus to all generations forever and ever. Amen.

— Journal —

Owning My Life
Why My Life Matters to God

Knowing I have only one life to live, one opportunity to invest it fully in the Kingdom of God, has given energy and purpose to each day and every season of my life.

SALLY CLARKSON (*DANCING WITH MY FATHER*)

_____

_____

_____

_____

_____

_____

_____

_____

_____

_____

_____

Sally Clarkson
Books and Resources to
Help You Own Your Life

Sally has served Christ in ministry for four decades. She and
Clay started Whole Heart Ministries in 1994 to serve Christian
parents. Since then, Sally has spoken to thousands of women
in her Mom Heart Conferences and written extensively about
motherhood, faith, and life. She is a regular mom blogger.

ONLINE
SallyClarkson.com — Personal blog for Christian women
MomHeart.com — Ministry blog for Christian mothers
WholeHeart.org — Ministry website, blog, and store
MomHeartConference.com — Ministry events website

IN PRINT BY SALLY
The Lifegiving Home (Tyndale Momentum)
The Lifegiving Home Experience (Tyndale Momentum)
Own Your Life (Tyndale Momentum)
You Are loved (with Angela Perritt, Tyndale Momentum)
10 Gifts of Wisdom (Whole Heart Press)
Desperate (with Sarah Mae, Thomas Nelson)
The Mom Walk (Whole Heart Press)
Dancing with My Father (WaterBrook Press)
The Ministry of Motherhood (WaterBrook Press)
The Mission of Motherhood (WaterBrook Press)
Seasons of a Mother's Heart (Apologia Press)

CONTACT INFORMATION
Whole Heart Ministries | Mom Heart Ministry
PO Box 3445 | Monument, CO 80132 | USA
719.488.4466 | 888.488.4HOME | 888.FAX.2WHM
whm@wholeheart.org | wholeheart@gmail.com

Made in the USA
Monee, IL
04 June 2021

70231431R00089